THE Word CHANGES EVERYTHING

Copyright © 2023 by Nora Shariff-Borden.
All rights reserved. This book or any portion thereof
may not be reproduced or used in any manner whatsoever
without the express written permission of the publisher
except for the use of brief quotations in a book review.

Printed in the United States of America

First Printing, 2023

THE WORD CHANGES EVERYTHING

BY DR. NORA SHARIFF-BORDEN

MY DEDICATION TO MY DEAR FRIEND REV. DR. STEPHANIE CASTRO

I dedicate this book to my dear friend Rev. Dr. Stephanie Castro. She is an amazing woman of God. She brings light into the lives of all those she has the privilege to meet.

I met this amazing woman 33 years ago. The moment I met her, I saw the greatness that God had placed inside of her. I knew He had great plans for her life and that she would do great things for the Kingdom of God.

What truly amazed me was her willingness to do anything for Him. A person who never says no to the Lord. This great woman of God has not had a life without challenges, but she has overcome them through the Grace of God.

I realize now it was because of the guidance of the Lord Jesus Christ in her life. And because of her faithfulness, He Blessed her with the love of her life Rev. Dr. Pastor Pedro. This great gift from God has loved her, comforted her, prayed with her, supported her, and encouraged her through it all. My dear and lovely friend, you are a gift from God.

THE WORD CHANGES EVERYTHING

I dedicate this book, *The Word Changes Everything*, to you, My Dear and Beautiful Friend Rev. Dr. Stephanie Castro.

I pray for the Lord's blessing upon your life now and through eternity.

Blessings.

Your Dear Friend,

Dr. Nora Shariff-Borden

TABLE OF CONTENTS

Message To Readers	11
Thank You	13
Preface	15
Author's Biography	17
A Blessed Woman Speaks In Confidence	21
All You Have to Do Is Believe	25
God Has Begun A Great Work In Me	29
God Has Given You The Power To Be Great	33
God Is My Shield	37
God Will Meet My Every Need	41
God's Plan For My Life	45
I Will Not Be Anxious	49
I Am A Blessed Woman	53
I Am A Capable, Intelligent, And Virtuous Woman	57
I Am Blessed	61
I Am Chosen	65
I Am Guided By The Lord	69
I Am Healed By His Blood	73
I Am Lacking Nothing	77
I Am Powerful	81

I Am Wonderfully Made By You	85
I Choose To Look At What Is Not Seen	89
I Give Thanks To The Lord	93
I Have Been Bought With A Price	97
I Have The Power To Get Wealth	101
I Hear You Lord	105
I Know The Voice Of God	109
I Must Ask	113
I Shall Seek God At All Times	117
I Speak Great Words From My Heart	121
I Walk In The Confidence Of The Lord	125
I Will Exhort The Lord Always	129
I Will Give My Troubles To The Lord	133
I Will Humble Myself Before The Lord	137
I Will Praise Him At All Times	141
I Will Seek The Lord At All Times	145
I Will Sing Praises To My God	149
I Will Trust In The Lord	153
I Will Wait Patiently On The Lord	157
Lord Help Me Fight The Good Fight	161
Lord Lead Me To Your Truth	165
Love Covers Everything	169
Loving Christ	173
My Circle Of Influence Is Key	177
My Confidence Is In Christ Jesus	181
My Gifts Have Power	185
My God Does Not Change	189
My God Is Working All Things Out For Me	193
My Help Comes From The Lord	197
My Light Is Shining Brightly	201
My Lord Is Strong And Mighty	205

My Lord's Mercy Endures Forever	209
My Lord Will Always Be With Me	213
My Mind Is Renewed	217
Scriptures to Inspire You	221
Quotes to Inspire You	224

A MESSAGE TO MY READERS

Thank you for purchasing this powerful book, *The Word Changes Everything*. Our words do have power. God intends to bless us through our words. Our words can make our lives become what God created us to be. I want you to see, feel and capture the very essence of the power of God's Word. It will transform your very life. Two of the most excellent books I have ever read are *The Bible* and *The Secret Power Within* by Dr. George D. Hamilton.

You may be asking why these two books. Well, I am glad you asked. *The Bible* is our blueprint for life. God created this manual for us to fulfill our purpose here on earth. *The Secret Power Within* shares that everything we desire resides inside us through the power of our words. Your words can allow you to live an abundant life 365 days a year or a life full of regrets all because of your words. So, the fact that you purchased this book tells me you are ready for a change in your life.

Writing this book for you has been a blessing to me. It has reminded me that God wants me to succeed in this life and that my birthright is to have whatever I want through the Power of Jesus Christ. I want you to know that you are destined for greatness. You may be asking yourself how I know this. Well, again, I am glad you asked. It is because God said so.

THE WORD CHANGES EVERYTHING

But don't just take my word. Look it up in your Manuel. (*The Bible*)

We all go through a period where we question whether this is or that is going to happen or whether God is really listening or even paying attention to our needs. Well, the answer is yes, He is. God only wants the best for you and me. He wants to see us reach our full potential in this life! In the book of Matthew, God tells us to let our light shine so brightly that others can see our good deeds and glorify our Father, who is in heaven.

Our words have the power to change our lives. That is why we must be careful about the words we speak. We must say only words that will make a difference in our lives and be careful not to allow others to speak negative words in our lives.

This tells me that every good thing we confess will manifest itself in our lives. I want you to know that your words change everything, and it will also open our eyes to the power of God's word. Remember, *The Word Changes Everything*! Enjoy!

Blessings,

Dr. Nora Shariff-Borden
Founder and CEO of BWOTMFG

THANK YOU

Thank You, Lord, for filling me with your words to write this powerful book, The Word Changes Everything. Thank You for showing me the power of your Word.

To my amazing mother, thank you for always believing in me and my visions! You were the epitome of greatness. Thank You for showing me the importance of working hard for what you want in life. I love and miss you. I wish you were here to see how your support and your love have helped me to become a very successful businesswoman. You raised four powerful and amazing daughters who love the Lord. Mother, you were definitely one of a kind.

To my beautiful sisters, thank you for all your prayers, support, and love

As always, I want to thank my amazing husband, who always supports me in everything I do. I love you to the moon and back.

To my children, my goal as your mother is to always be the example in your life that God has called me to be. I love you, and I am so very proud of you and thankful to God for choosing me to be your mother.

THE WORD CHANGES EVERYTHING

To my beautiful grandchildren, you inspire me. I love you with the love of Christ. Know that all things are possible for you through the power of Christ.

To my amazing and powerful pastor, the Rev Dr. Cynthia Hale, who pushed through all those who did not believe you were qualified to pastor or preach the Word of God. Thank you for being so confident in yourself and the vision that God has given you. I have learned so much from you; thank you for teaching us that we can do anything we desire If we are willing to work and pay the price for our dreams.

Thank You, Stephane Hunt, for always saying yes when I ask you to work on another book project. Love you with the love of Christ.

Sonia, I thank God for you every day! You are indeed the best of the best. Thanks for always having my back.

Aishah, working with you as a mother-and-daughter team is a pleasure. You are such a ray of light in my life. Thank You!

Thank You to my dear friend Nancy Pettaway for inspiring me with the title of this powerful book, *The Word Changes Everything*.

PREFACE

The Word Changes Everything is a powerful book that shows how the Word of God changes everything in your life for the better. The enemy does not want us to study God's Word because he recognizes that God gave us this great manual (called the Bible) so that we would know the great power we have to overcome - anything that gets in our way. God tells us to meditate on His word day and night. To me, that means studying it. Did you know anything you study you become master at it?

The Word of God empowers us with wisdom, knowledge, and understanding; most importantly, it shows us how much God loves His people and wants them to succeed. I want you to wake up every morning reminding yourself that *The Word Changes Everything*.

NORA SHARIFF-BORDEN

Dr. Nora Shariff-Borden and her three younger sisters were born and raised in Boston, Massachusetts. Nora and her husband, Neil, live outside Atlanta, Georgia. Together they have six adult children, 14 grandchildren, and three great-grandchildren. The seed of Christianity was planted in her life by her Grandmother, Nora Dunn.

Nora moved away from the Lord and became a Muslim. Once she woke up and realized an emptiness that was in her spirit, and that she missed her Lord and Savior, Jesus Christ. God saw fit to bring her back to Him over 30 years ago, and she accepted her call from God to become a Christian inspirational speaker.

Nora founded Business Women On The Move For God (BWOTMFG). This organization inspires and encourages people to be who God has called them to be, which is awesome, powerful, mighty, and great. God wants them to be clear about their goals and dreams and how to achieve them through Him. Nora started BWOTMFG because she loves seeing people own their greatness and learn how to walk in it daily! She wants the next generation of young people to realize their greatness and be unapologetic about it. Nora wants people to be able to get up when they have fallen and to learn the importance of continuing their journey! She wants them to be bold about their relationship with their Lord Jesus Christ.

Dr. Nora is the Founder and CEO of Spiritual Touch TV, where she hosts a weekly online show, Real Conversations with Nora, which focuses on the many issues that people face every day through transparent conversations. Nora digs deep to help people talk about their issues to help them reclaim their authentic selves and overcome their obstacles so they can navigate through life successfully. Most importantly, the interviewers have a good time!

Nora believes she has a gift from God that allows her to connect with God's people. She believes that if you can touch the heart of people, they will do all they can to support you. Nora's goal is to teach people that their words have the power to change their lives. She also believes she can help them paint a picture of what they want their life to look like so that when it appears, all they have to do is step into it.

Nora is a woman with a serious mission who believes that if she meets true needs of God's people with total sincerity and commitment to serve as God has called her to do, her work will not be in vain.

Nora is the visionary of Powerful Women United Worldwide (PWUW). The mission of PWUW is to empower and support women of all backgrounds, ages, and walks of life to achieve their full potential. This group strives to create a safe and inclusive space where women can connect, learn, and grow together and where their unique voices and contributions are valued and celebrated.

In March of 2022, Nora was bestowed an Honorary Doctorate Degree from Trinity International University ofAmbassadors (TIUA).

THE WORD CHANGES EVERYTHING

On December 3rd of, 2022, she received the Presidential Lifetime Achievement Award, Also, in February of 2023, in honor of Black History Month Dr. Nora was awarded The Presidential Legacy Lifetime Achievement Award from Trinity International University of Ambassadors, in honor of our 44th President, Barack Obama.
June of 2023, she was awarded The International Anthology of the Year Award by TIUA School of Business for Your Faith Will Make You Unstoppable.

Her future projects for BWOTMFG include developing a program called Teen Tv Media and establishing a $10,000 scholarship program for young women who major in business.

Dr. Nora Believes that "Great things happen when people have Great Expectations!"

Stay in touch with Dr. Nora Shariff-Borden and Business Women On The Move For God by following along at:
Instagram @bwotmfg
Facebook @BusinessWomenontheMoveforGod
YouTube @NoraShariff3505

You can also visit https://www.bwotmfg.com/.

Dr. Nora Shariff-Borden
Founder and CEO of BWOTMFG
Stone Mountain, GA
470-553-4107
info@bwotmfg.com

CHAPTER 1

THE WORD CHANGES EVERYTHING

A BLESSED WOMAN SPEAKS IN CONFIDENCE

THE WORD CHANGES EVERYTHING

> Blessed is the woman who fills her quiver with them!
> She shall not be put to shame when she speaks with her enemies
> in the gate. Psalm 127:5

As a blessed woman, I speak with confidence because I know that I am loved and valued by my Creator. I am grateful for the many blessings in my life, including the people who support and encourage me, the opportunities that come my way, and the strength and courage that I must have when facing life's challenges.

I am confident in my abilities and skills, and I know that I have something to offer the world. I am not afraid to take risks and try new things, even if they are outside of my comfort zone. I believe in myself and my potential, and I am willing to put in the hard work and dedication necessary to achieve my goals.

At the same time, I am humble and recognize that I am not perfect. I make mistakes, and I am constantly learning and growing from them. I am open to feedback, and I use it to improve myself and my work.

Overall, as a blessed woman, I am confident in who I am, what I stand for, and what I can achieve. I trust in my faith and my journey, and I know that I am on the right path toward fulfilling my purpose and living a fulfilling life.

God has blessed me to speak with His confidence. And I am committed to walking in the confidence of the Lord.

THE WORD CHANGES EVERYTHING

Do you need to increase your confidence in God?

If so, how?

Are you confident in your skills?

Do you realize that you are not perfect?

Are you totally confident in who you are?

> **Prayer:** Lord, thank You for allowing me to see the importance of being in your presence. Thank you for allowing me to discern your presence. Thank you for the many gifts you have blessed me with. I am so thankful to be guided by you.

CHAPTER 2

THE WORD CHANGES EVERYTHING

ALL YOU HAVE TO DO IS BELIEVE

THE WORD CHANGES EVERYTHING

All things are possible for those who believe Mark 9:24

Belief is a powerful force that can shape our thoughts, feelings, and actions. When we believe in something, it can give us the strength and motivation to pursue our goals, overcome obstacles, and make positive changes in our lives.

However, belief alone is not always enough to achieve our desired outcomes. We also need to take our beliefs and connect them to our actions and work towards our goals, using our beliefs as a source of inspiration and guidance.

Additionally, it's important to note that not all beliefs are created equal. Some beliefs may be based on misinformation, superstition, or prejudice, which can lead us down the wrong path. It's important to critically evaluate our beliefs and seek out evidence and information that supports them. As believers, we must do as Matthew 6:33 tells us to Seek first the Kingdom of God and His righteousness, and all things will be given to you.

Overall, while belief can be a powerful tool for achieving our goals and living a fulfilling life, it's important to balance it with thinking positively and taking the necessary steps of action.

THE WORD CHANGES EVERYTHING

Do you believe in your God-given Power? Be honest with your answer.

If so, how.

If not, why.

Are you connecting your beliefs with your actions?

Are you seeking the Lord for guidance?

> **Prayer:** Lord, thank You for helping me to see that I need to believe that all things are possible if I believe and take action toward my dreams. Lord, I am determined to walk and believe in the greatness You have blessed me with.

CHAPTER 3

THE WORD CHANGES EVERYTHING

GOD HAS BEGUN A GREAT WORK IN ME

THE WORD CHANGES EVERYTHING

And I am sure of this, that He who began a good work in you will bring it to completion at the day of Jesus Christ Philippians 1:6

Beginning a new work within yourself requires a combination of self-reflection, planning, and action. The most important thing is to seek the power of God to guide you as you begin this new journey of identifying who you are or want to become.

Identify the area of growth: Begin by identifying the area of your life where you want to see growth. This could be personal, professional, or spiritual development. Take the time to seek God and ask Him when you need to change; trust me, He will reveal it to you.

Reflect on your motivations: It is important to reflect on your motivations for wanting to grow in this area. What are your goals? What do you hope to gain from this work? Understanding your motivations will help keep you focused and motivated. This is a time when you can sit quietly before the Lord to hear His voice as He begins to move you in the direction, He has for you.

Set goals: Set specific, measurable goals that will help you achieve the growth you desire. Break down larger goals into medium and smaller ones which will be more manageable.

Create a plan: Create a plan for how you will achieve your goals. This could include specific actions you will take, resources you will use, and a timeline for completion. Deadlines are crucial!

Taking action: Begin taking action towards your goals. This may involve trying new things, seeking out new experiences, or working on developing specific skills or habits. It may all so be a time to step out on faith and become a risk-taker.

Evaluate your progress: Regularly evaluate your progress towards your goals. Celebrate your successes, even the small ones, and adjust your approach as needed to stay on track.

Remember that personal growth is a process and requires patience, persistence, and self-compassion. Be kind to yourself as you work towards your goals and remember that setbacks are a natural part of the process.

Remember this, God has begun a great work in you, and He will bring it to completion.

THE WORD CHANGES EVERYTHING

Are you ready to be a risk-taker?

How often do you sit quietly to hear from God?

Do you believe that God is beginning a good work in you?

What areas have you identified that you need to grow in?

> **Prayer:** Lord, help me to realize that You have begun a new work in me and that You are faithful to bring it to completion. And that all things are possible if I just believe in Your power that is at work within me.

CHAPTER 4

THE WORD CHANGES EVERYTHING

GOD HAS GIVEN YOU THE POWER TO BE GREAT

THE WORD CHANGES EVERYTHING

I tell you the truth, whatever you bind on earth will be bound in heaven, and whatever you loose on earth will be loosed in heaven. Matthew 18:18

There is so much packed into this scripture. It says to me that God has given me the power to control how my life turns out.

The key is you must have a positive mindset and believe in your own potential. Believing in yourself is an important step to achieving greatness. However, it's important to remember that greatness often requires hard work, dedication, and perseverance. Setting specific goals and developing a plan to achieve them can help you realize your full potential and reach the level of greatness that you aspire to. Don't be afraid to ask for help along the way and to learn from your mistakes. With the right mindset and a willingness to put in the effort, you can achieve great things.

Believing in yourself and your abilities is the first step toward achieving greatness. It's important to identify your strengths and weaknesses and work on improving yourself consistently. Setting goals and taking actionable steps toward achieving them is also crucial.

Every person has the potential to achieve greatness in their own unique way. It may take hard work, dedication, and perseverance, but with the right mindset and effort, you can accomplish great things. Why? Because God said so!

Remember, greatness is not just about achieving success or fame but also about making a positive impact on the world and the people around you. So, keep pushing yourself to be the best version of yourself and always strive to make a difference in the world.

THE WORD CHANGES EVERYTHING

However, it's important to remember that greatness doesn't come overnight or without hard work and dedication. It takes consistent effort and a willingness to learn and improve over time. So, continue to cultivate that positive attitude and pair it with intentional action toward your goals. Have confidence in your ability to be blessed on your journey toward greatness! And you will succeed!

THE WORD CHANGES EVERYTHING

Do you believe that God has given you the power to be great?

Are you confident about your journey to greatness?

What does today's scripture say to you?

Are you up for the hard work that it takes to receive the greatness that God has for you?

Remember, faith without work is dead. Which says you must work hard for what you want out of life.

Prayer: Father, help me to see the importance of working hard for my dreams and goals. Help me see that I must keep my eyes on You at all times and that I must seek Your power.

CHAPTER 5

THE WORD CHANGES EVERYTHING

GOD IS MY SHIELD

THE WORD CHANGES EVERYTHING

> But no weapon that is formed against you shall prosper, and every tongue that shall rise against you in judgment you shall show to be in the wrong. The peace, the righteousness, security, triumph over opposition is the heritage of the servants of the Lord. Isaiah 54:17

God is my shield against negative thoughts, fears, and uncertainties and can help provide a sense of purpose and meaning in my life. It is important to recognize that taking God as your shield is a deeply personal and subjective experience; it can be helpful to explore and reflect on your beliefs and how they inform your worldview and actions. Additionally, seeking support from a trusted community or spiritual leader can provide further guidance and insight into your faith journey.

Deepen your understanding: Spend time studying and reflecting on the teachings of the word of God. Read scriptures and ask God to give you understanding where you have none. Have confidence that He will reveal His word to you.

Develop a daily practice: Incorporate practices such as prayer and meditating on the word of God into your daily routine. This can help you stay connected to God and His word. This helps you build a sense of inner strength and resilience.

Connect with a community: Surround yourself with people who share your beliefs and values. Join a faith-based community or group where you can find support, encouragement, and fellowship.

Practice gratitude: Cultivate a mindset of gratitude and focus on the blessings in your life. This can help you stay positive and hopeful even in difficult times. Know this God did not tell us that the weapon wouldn't

THE WORD CHANGES EVERYTHING

come, but He promised that they would not prosper.

Remember that making faith your shield of protection is a journey, and it takes time and effort to develop a deep and meaningful connection to your beliefs. Be patient with yourself and keep taking steps towards strengthening your faith in God's word.

Do you believe that God is your shield?

What does it mean to you that no weapon formed against you shall prosper?

Are you trusting God along this journey of your life?

> **Prayer:** Lord, thank You for not letting the weapons formed against me prosper. I have confidence in Your power to protect me. And every tongue that shall rise against me. Lord, I love You and appreciate all that You do for me.

CHAPTER 6

THE WORD CHANGES EVERYTHING

GOD WILL MEET MY EVERY NEED

THE WORD CHANGES EVERYTHING

> And My God will supply every need of yours according to His riches in glory in Christ Jesus. To our God and father be glory forever and ever. Amen. Philippians 4:19-20

The belief that God will meet our every need is what we believe as Christians. It is often rooted in the idea that God is responsible for providing for our needs and that we can trust His power to take care of us.

While this can bring comfort and a sense of security, it's important to remember that it doesn't mean that we just sit around and do nothing. It is important that we take responsibility and actions and use the gifts that God has blessed us with. It is important to make choices that support our wellbeing and help us achieve our life desires.

The idea of God meeting our every need can be interpreted in different ways depending on where one is in their spiritual walk. For example, some might interpret it to mean that God will provide material wealth or financial abundance, while others might view it as more spiritual or emotional support.

When you believe that God will meet your every need, it's important to cultivate a sense of trust and faith in the power of God, as well as take practical steps to care for yourself and those around us, which is one of the greatest gifts God has given us.

THE WORD CHANGES EVERYTHING

Do you trust that God meets your every need?

Do you feel comfortable in God's power?

What are the ways you believe that God will supply your every need?

Are you making decisions that support your well-being?

> **Prayer:** Lord, thank You for meeting all my needs and for being the one that protects and guides me in all areas of my life. Thank You for showing me the way I should go, Lord; I trust Your amazing power over my life.

CHAPTER 7

THE WORD CHANGES EVERYTHING

GOD'S PLANS FOR MY LIFE

THE WORD CHANGES EVERYTHING

For I know the thought and plans that I have for you, says the Lord, thought and plans for welfare and peace and not for evil, to give you hope in your final outcome.

Then you will call upon Me, and you will come and pray to Me, and I will hear and heed you.

Then you will seek Me, inquire, for, and require Me, necessity (as a vital necessity) and find Me when you search for Me with all your heart.
Jeremiah 29:11-13

As Christians, we believe God has a plan for our lives and seeking to understand that plan can be a powerful motivator for personal growth and fulfillment.

Seek guidance: Prayer and meditation can help you connect with God and clarify your purpose and direction. Listen to the inner voice of the Holy Spirit and pay attention to signs that He is sending you as He shows the way you should take.

Use your talents: God has given each of us unique talents and abilities and using them to serve others can be a fulfilling and meaningful way to live out your purpose.

Serve others: Serving others is an important aspect for as Christians, it can help us make a positive impact on the world. Look for ways to help those in need and contribute to our community.

Trust in God's timing: Sometimes, God's plans for our lives may not unfold in the way or at the pace we expect. Trusting in God's timing and having patience can help you to stay focused and remain open to opportunities as they arise.

Embrace change: Life is full of changes, and sometimes God's plans for us may require us to step out of our comfort zone or make difficult choices. Embracing change and having faith that God will guide you can help you to navigate through challenging times.

Remember, God's plan for your life may be different from what you expect, but by seeking guidance, using your talents, serving others, trusting in God's timing, and embracing change, you can live a purposeful and fulfilling life.

THE WORD CHANGES EVERYTHING

Are you trusting God's plans for your life?

Are you willing to embrace the changes that life brings your way?

How willing are you to trust God's timing?

Are you using the gifts that God has blessed you with?

Prayer: Lord, thank You for all the gifts You have blessed me with. Thank You for showing me the importance of serving others. Thank You for showing me that Your timing is everything and that I need to just wait on it.

CHAPTER 8

THE WORD CHANGES EVERYTHING

I WILL NOT BE ANXIOUS

THE WORD CHANGES EVERYTHING

> Do not be anxious about anything, but in everything by prayer and supplication with thanksgiving let your request be made known to God! And the peace of God, which surpasses all understanding, will guard your heart and your minds in Christ Jesus. Philippians 4:6-7

I love God's word. He gives us clear instructions to deal with anything that might interfere with the great plans He has for us. He is letting us know that we don't have to be anxious about anything because He got us in the palm of His hand where we can feel totally secure. Here are some additional great tips for focusing on not being anxious.

Practice Deep Breathing: When you feel anxious, taking deep breaths can help calm your nervous system and reduce your anxiety. Exercise regularly: Exercise can help reduce feelings of anxiety and improve your overall mood.

Get Enough Sleep: Lack of sleep can contribute to feelings of anxiety. Make sure you're getting enough sleep each night.

Practice Mindfulness: Mindfulness techniques can help you stay present and reduce anxious thoughts.

Challenge Negative Thoughts: When you start to feel anxious, try to identify any negative thoughts that may be contributing to your anxiety. Challenge those thoughts and replace them with more positive ones.

Seek Support: If your anxiety is affecting your daily life, consider reaching out to a mental health professional for support.

Managing anxiety is a process and it takes time and effort to overcome it!

THE WORD CHANGES EVERYTHING

But know this, when you follow God's instructions, He will calm down your anxiety.

But with patience and persistence, you can learn to manage your anxiety and live a fulfilling life.

What are you anxious about?

Are you ready to surrender it to God?

Do you believe that all things are possible when trusting in God?

Have you given all your problems over to God?

> **Prayer:** Lord, thank You for helping me through these trying times. I trust that all things are working together for my good because of Your working power that is at work in my life. Lord, Thank You for helping me to always keep my eyes on You because You are the fixer.

CHAPTER 9

THE WORD CHANGES EVERYTHING

I AM A BLESSED WOMAN

> Blessed Is the Woman who believes in, trust in, and relies on the Lord, and whose hope and confidence is in the lord. Jeremiah 17:7

Being a blessed woman often involves cultivating certain virtues and behaviors that are believed to be pleasing to God or beneficial to oneself and others. Some of these virtues may include:

Gratitude: Being grateful for what one has in life, rather than focusing on what one lacks, is believed to attract blessings and positive energy.

Compassion: Showing kindness and empathy towards others, especially those who are less fortunate or struggling, is seen as a way of earning blessings from the Lord.

Humility: Recognizing one's limitations and being willing to learn from others, as well as acknowledging one's successes and blessings as gifts rather than accomplishments of one's own making.

Faith: Believing in the power of God and trusting His goodness and wisdom is seen as a way of opening oneself up to blessings and divine guidance.

Service: Helping others in various ways, whether through volunteering, donating money or time, or simply being a good listener or friend, is often seen as a way of earning blessings and living a purposeful life.

In addition to cultivating these virtues, being a blessed woman may also involve practices such as prayer, meditation, and fasting. Ultimately, being a blessed woman is about living a life of purpose, meaningful, and fulfillment and contributing positively to the world around us.

THE WORD CHANGES EVERYTHING

How do you consider yourself blessed?

Recognizing one's limitations and being willing to learn from others keep us humble.

What are your thoughts?

Believing in the power of God and trusting His goodness and wisdom is seen as a way of opening oneself up to blessings and divine guidance.

What are your thoughts?

How important is it to you to serve others?

> **Prayer:** Lord, thank You for showing me how Blessed I am. Thank You for showing me the importance of a grateful heart. Thank You for Loving me even in my weakness.

CHAPTER 10

THE WORD CHANGES EVERYTHING

I AM A CAPABLE, INTELLIGENT, AND VIRTUOUS WOMAN

THE WORD CHANGES EVERYTHING

A capable, intelligent, and virtuous woman-who is he who can find her. She is far more precious than jewels, and her value is far above rubies or pearls.

The heart of her husband trusts in her confidently and relies on and believes in her securely so that he has no lack of gain or need of dishonest spoil.

She comforts, encourages, and does him only good as long as there is life within her.

She seeks out wool and flax and works with willing hands to develop it.
Proverbs 31: 10-13

Becoming a capable, intelligent, and virtuous woman requires dedication, effort, and a willingness to learn and grow.

Set goals: Set specific, achievable goals for yourself in areas that you want to improve. This could be academic, professional, personal, or even spiritual goals. Write them down and keep track of your progress. Make sure you set a deadline for those goals.

Develop your skills: Identify your strengths and weaknesses and work on improving your skills. This could be through formal education, online courses, or learning from mentors and experts in your field.

Cultivate good habits: Cultivate good habits that will help you achieve your goals. This could include habits such as regularly reading the word of God, exercising, healthy eating, and time management, and connecting with like-minded people.

THE WORD CHANGES EVERYTHING

Stay informed: Stay connected with the word of God will help you to stay focused and informed.

Seek out mentors: Seek out mentors who can guide and advise you on your journey. Look for people who are successful in areas that you want to improve in and ask them for guidance.

Practice self-care: Taking care of yourself is crucial for your mental and physical well-being. Make sure to take breaks, get enough sleep, and do activities that bring you joy.

Give back: Giving back to your community can be a rewarding experience and can help you develop your leadership skills.

Remember, becoming a capable, intelligent, and virtuous woman is a journey, not a destination. Continuously work on improving yourself and stay open to learning and growth.

THE WORD CHANGES EVERYTHING

Do you enjoy giving back to your community?

Are you good at taking care of yourself spiritually, emotionally, and healthily?

How do you stay focused when you feel off course?

Do you have a mentor in your life?

> **Prayer:** Lord, thank You for helping me become all that You have called me to be. I am thankful that I have become a capable, Intelligent, And Virtuosi Woman!

CHAPTER 11

THE WORD CHANGES EVERYTHING

I AM BLESSED

THE WORD CHANGES EVERYTHING

The Lord bless you keep you; The Lord make His face to shine upon you and be gracious to you; The Lord lifts up His countenance upon you and give you peace. Numbers 6:24-26

"Blessed" can mean different things to different people, but it generally refers to feeling grateful, fortunate, or favored by the God of this universe.

Cultivate an attitude of gratitude: Focus on the good things in your life and express gratitude for them regularly. This can be as simple as saying "thank you" to someone who helps you, keeping a gratitude journal, or practicing gratitude and meditating on the word of God!

Be kind to others: Acts of kindness can help create positive energy and attract blessings. Look for ways to help others, whether it's volunteering, offering a kind word, or simply listening when someone needs to talk like God does with us.

Stay positive: Try to maintain a positive attitude even when things aren't going well. This can be challenging, but a positive mindset can help you see the silver lining in difficult situations and keep you moving forward. This is a time that allows you to remember how blessed you really are!

Trust the process: Sometimes, we don't understand why things are happening, but we trust that everything is happening for a reason. Keep your faith strong and believe that God is working everything out for your good!

Stay connected to your Faith in God's Power: When you have faith in God's power to work all things out for your good, it helps you to stay connected to that source of power! Whether it's prayer, meditating on God's word, or walking by faith, stay committed to it. This can help you feel more connected to God! It is so good to know that the maker of heaven and earth will bring you a sense of peace and purpose in your life.

Do you stop and thank God for the blessing that He sends your way?

Are you focused on the blessing of God or your circumstance?

How willing are you to trust the process God is taking you through?

Do you find it hard or easy to stay positive?

> **Prayer:** Lord, I thank You for showing me that I am blessed and highly favored with Your love! You make all things right in my life even when I can't see them! I am so blessed and grateful to have You in my life. Help me to remember that I am blessed no matter what is going on in my life!

CHAPTER 12

THE WORD CHANGES EVERYTHING

I AM CHOSEN

THE WORD CHANGES EVERYTHING

A good name is to be chosen rather than great riches, and favor is better than silver and gold. Proverbs 22:1

Hopefully, when you were born, your parents chose a name with great meaning. This allows you to connect with the meaning of your great name. My name means light! I have decided to take that everywhere I go and to bring a shade of light with me. This is my interpretation of the name Nora.

Choosing a name is one of the most important decisions a parent can make for their child. A name is not just a label; it is an identity, a representation of one's culture, heritage, and family history. Choosing a name that holds great value and explore some factors to consider when making this decision.

Body: Importance of a name: A name is an integral part of one's identity and can impact a person's self-esteem and confidence. It can reflect one's cultural background, family history, and personal values. A name can also influence how a person is perceived by others and can have an impact on their social interactions.

These are factors to consider when choosing a name:

Cultural significance: Consider the cultural background and significance of the name. Does it reflect the family's heritage and values? Unique but not too unusual: Choosing a unique name can help a child stand out, but it should not be too unusual that it causes difficulties in pronunciation or spelling.

Future implications: Consider how the name may impact the child's future opportunities, such as in their profession or social interactions.

Family history: Choosing a name that has a family history and can add sentimental value and honor to previous generations.

Increased Self-worth: A name that holds great value can boost a child's self-worth and instill a sense of pride in their identity and heritage.

Sense of belonging: A name that reflects one's cultural background and family history can provide a sense of belonging and connection to their roots.

Positive impact on social interactions: A name that is well-known or carries positive associations can have a positive impact on how a child is perceived by others.

In conclusion, choosing a name with great value is a crucial decision that can impact a child's identity, self-worth, and future opportunities. Factors to consider include cultural significance, uniqueness, future implications, and family history. A name that holds great value can provide a sense of belonging, boost one's self-esteem, and positively impact social interactions.

THE WORD CHANGES EVERYTHING

How do you feel about the name that was chosen for you?

Does your name bring pride?

Do you know the meaning of your name?

Do you feel like it brings you a sense of family value?

Prayer: Father, thank You for showing me that my name has value to You. Thank you for letting me know that before I was formed in my mother's womb, you knew me. I am so thankful that I am great in the sight of Your eyes.

CHAPTER 13

THE WORD CHANGES EVERYTHING

I AM GUIDED BY THE LORD

> I instruct you and teach you the way you should go I will watch over and I will guide you with my eyes. Psalms 32:8

Taking instructions from God can mean different things to different people depending on where they are with their faith. The scripture gives us a clear explanation that God will guide us.

Prayer and Meditation: Spend time in prayer, and meditation to connect with God. This will help you clear your mind of distractions and allow you to reflect on who God is. It will help you slow down and listen to the voice of God.

Read Sacred Texts: Read and study the word of God. The Bible will help you gain a deeper understanding of God's teachings and what He expects of you.

Seek guidance from spiritual leaders: Seek guidance from your spiritual leaders, such as pastors; they may have insights into how to discern God's will for your life.

Practice discernment: Practice discernment to distinguish God's voice from other thoughts and influences. This involves being attentive to your thoughts and feelings and learning to recognize the still, small voice of God.

Live a virtuous life: Strive to live a virtuous life by following God's word and teachings. This will help you to be more receptive to God's guidance and better able to discern His will.

Remember that hearing from God is a personal and subjective experience.

THE WORD CHANGES EVERYTHING

It may take time and effort to discern God's voice, but with practice, you can develop a deeper relationship with God and learn to trust His guidance.

Are you open to instructions from the Lord?

How do you practice discerning God's voice?

Are you open to seeking Godly wisdom?

Do you realize that praying and meditating on God's word is key in our lives?

Prayer: Lord, thank You for allowing me to see the importance of being in Your presence. Thank You for allowing me to decern Your presence. Thank You for the many gifts You have blessed me with. I am so thankful to be guided by You.

CHAPTER 14

THE WORD CHANGES EVERYTHING

I AM HEALED BY HIS BLOOD

> But He was bruised for our iniquities; the chastisement of our peace was upon Him; and with His Stripes we are healed. Isaiah 53:5

Spiritual ailments. This belief is often associated with spiritual belief and is grounded in the belief that God is all-powerful and compassionate.

Recognize that belief is a personal choice: Believing in God's healing is a personal choice; some people may find comfort in it, while others may not. It is essential to respect each person's beliefs and choices. The best thing you can do for them is plant the seed of Christ in their lives.

Have faith and trust in God: Believing in God's healing requires having faith and trust that God can heal. This faith can be strengthened through prayer, reading the word of God, and participating in fellowship with other believers.

Seek medical treatment: While believing in God's healing power, it is crucial to seek medical treatment for any physical or mental health issues. Medical treatment can work in conjunction with spiritual practices to promote healing. God tells us that by His stripes, we are healed.

Practice gratitude and positive thinking: Focusing on positive thoughts and practicing gratitude can help in promoting healing. It can help in shifting your focus from negative thoughts to positive ones. It can provide feelings of hope and optimism.

Be patient: Healing is a process, and it may not happen overnight. Having patience and trust in God's timing is essential. It is also essential to remember that God is in the healing business.

THE WORD CHANGES EVERYTHING

In summary, believing in God's healing involves having faith and trust in God's power to heal. While it is a personal choice, it can be practiced through prayer, positive thinking, and gratitude. It is also essential to seek medical treatment and have patience during the healing process.

How Patient are you with the things of God?

Do you believe in the power of God's healing?

Do you recognize that belief is a personal choice?

Do you have faith and trust God for your healing?

> **Prayer:** Lord, I thank You for my healing. It is by Your stripes that I am healed. Thank You for letting me know that You were bruised for my iniquities; the chastisement of my peace was upon You, and with Your Stripes, I am healed.

CHAPTER 15

THE WORD CHANGES EVERYTHING

I AM LACKING NOTHING

So that you are not lacking in any gift, as you wait for the revealing of the Lord Jesus Christ, who will sustain you to the end guiltless in the day of our Lord Jesus Christ. God is faithful, by whom you were called into the fellowship of his Son, Jesus Christ our Lord. 1 Corinthians 1:7-9

Creating an attitude of lacking nothing requires a shift in mindset and perspective. It involves cultivating a sense of abundance and gratitude for what one has rather than focusing on what is missing or lacking.

Practice gratitude: Focus on what you already have and express. gratitude for it. Write down at least three things you're grateful for each day. This helps you to shift your attention to what you have rather than what you lack.

Avoid comparison: Comparison is the thief of joy. Instead of comparing yourself to others and what you are lacking, focus on your own progress and growth. Celebrate your successes and learn from your failures.

Live within your means: Don't spend more than you have or buy things you don't need. Living within your means helps you to appreciate what you have and avoid unnecessary stress and debt.

Adopt a growth mindset: Believe that you can learn and grow from challenges and setbacks. See them as opportunities for growth and development rather than as failures. And know that all things work together for those who love God and are called to His purpose. And in Christ Jesus, we are not lacking in anything.

Focus on what you can control: Don't waste energy on things you can't control. Instead, focus on what you can control, such as your attitude and actions.

By practicing gratitude, avoiding comparison, living within your means, adopting a growth mindset, and focusing on what you can control, you can create an attitude of lacking nothing.

Do you feel like you are lacking?

How do you avoid thinking lack?

Do you find it hard not to compare yourself to others?

How do you overcome challenges and setbacks?

Prayer: Lord, thank You for showing me that in You, I have no lack and that with You, all things are possible. Lord, I appreciate You, Lord; I love You, and I trust You with all aspects of my life.

CHAPTER 16

THE WORD CHANGES EVERYTHING

I AM POWERFUL

THE WORD CHANGES EVERYTHING

> Now to Him who is able to do far more abundantly than all that we ask or think, according to the power at work within us. To him be glory in the church and in Christ Jesus throughout all generations, forever and ever. Amen. Ephesians 3:20-21

Recognizing your power is an important step towards personal growth and achieving our goals.

Accept and own your strengths: Start by identifying your strengths and acknowledging them. It's easy to focus on our weaknesses, but when we acknowledge our strengths, we begin to recognize the power which Christ gives us!

Focus on what you can control: Instead of worrying about things you can't control, leave those things for God to handle. When you focus on the things that you can control, you gain the power to change your attitude, your mindset, and your actions.

Celebrate your accomplishments: Celebrate your accomplishments, no matter how small they are. Recognizing your achievements will help you build confidence and recognize your own power.

Trust yourself: Trust your instincts and intuition. You know yourself better than anyone else, and you have the power to make decisions that are right for you. Remember, God has given you that power!

Embrace challenges: Embrace challenges and obstacles as opportunities for growth. Remember that you have the power to overcome any obstacle that comes your way.

THE WORD CHANGES EVERYTHING

Take action: Taking action is a powerful way to recognize your own power. When you take action, you're taking control of your life and making things happen. Most importantly, you are not handing your power over to others.

Remember that recognizing your own power is a journey, and it takes time. Learn to take steps each day in the direction that God wants to take you.

THE WORD CHANGES EVERYTHING

What steps are you taking to own your power?

Do you find it hard to embrace your challenges?

Are you taking time to celebrate your accomplishments?

Are you focusing on what you can control? And leave what you can't control in the hands of God?

> **Prayer:** Lord, help me trust You with all my concerns. Help me to know that You are in total control of my life. I am so grateful that You have my whole life in Your hands.

CHAPTER 17

THE WORD CHANGES EVERYTHING

———————

I AM WONDERFULLY MADE BY YOU

THE WORD CHANGES EVERYTHING

For You formed my inward parts; you knitted me together in my mother's womb. I praise you, for I am fearfully and wonderfully made. Wonderful are you works; my soul knows it very well. Pslam139:13-14

The idea of being wonderfully made by God comes from the Bible, specifically from Psalm 139:14, which says, "I praise you because I am fearfully and wonderfully made; your works are wonderful, I know that full well."

This verse reminds us that God has created each of us uniquely and with a purpose and that we should praise Him for this.

The concept of being wonderfully made by God also highlights the value and dignity of every human being, regardless of their race, gender, or abilities. It is a reminder that we are all precious in God's eyes and that we should treat ourselves and others with the same respect and love.

Furthermore, being wonderfully made by God also implies that we have a responsibility to take care of ourselves and our bodies. We should strive to live healthy lifestyles, both physically and spiritually, and treat our bodies as temples of the Holy Spirit.

In summary, the idea of being wonderfully made by God reminds us of our uniqueness, value, and responsibility to take care of ourselves and others. It is a reminder to praise God for His creation and to treat ourselves and others with love and respect.

THE WORD CHANGES EVERYTHING

Are you confident that God knew you before you formed in your mother's womb?

What are your thoughts on Psalm 139:14?

Do you recognize how wonderful you are?

Are you totally confident in who you are in Christ?

Prayer: Lord, thank You for all that You do to show me who I am in You! Thank You, for delivering me from sin and loving me even when I have sinned.

CHAPTER 18

THE WORD CHANGES EVERYTHING

I CHOOSE NOT TO FOCUS ON WHAT IS NOT SEEN

THE WORD CHANGES EVERYTHING

> While we look not at the things which are seen, but the things which are not seen: for the things which are seen are temporal; but the things which are not seen are eternal. 2 Corinthians 4:18

Have you ever heard the phrase, "out of sight, out of mind"? It's a common saying that suggests that when something is not visible or tangible, it's easy to forget about it. However, there's another way to look at things that are not seen. This is called walking by faith and not by sight. The key is to keep your focus on God.

Focusing on what is not seen can cause unnecessary stress, anxiety, and worry. It's easy to get caught up in "what if" scenarios and let your imagination run wild with all the possible negative outcomes. But when you choose not to focus on what is not seen, you can redirect your energy toward what is in your control and what you can do in the present moment. This allows you to give everything to God, who is the one who can handle all things.

For example, let's say you're worried about your job security. You're not sure if your company is going to downsize, and you're afraid that you might lose your job. Focusing on this possibility can cause you to feel anxious and stressed, even though you don't know for sure what's going to happen. But one thing you can be sure of is that God knows the plans He has for you, so there is no need to worry about things you have no control over.

In summary, choosing not to focus on what is not seen can help you reduce stress and anxiety and allow you to redirect your energy toward what you can control. It doesn't mean that you should ignore potential risks or challenges, but rather than letting them consume your thoughts and emotions, you can take proactive steps to prepare yourself for the great future God has for you.

Are you one of those people who has to always be in control?

Do you feel like you can walk by faith and not by sight?

Are you a risk taker?

Do you focus on what you see vs. what you do not see?

> **Prayer:** Lord, help me to keep my focus on You and not the things I see or do not see. Help me to remember that You work all things out for my good, because I love you and I am called according to Your purpose for my life.

CHAPTER 19

THE WORD CHANGES EVERYTHING

I GIVE THANKS TO THE LORD

THE WORD CHANGES EVERYTHING

> Let them thank the Lord for His steadfast love, for His wondrous works to the children of man! For He satisfies the Longing soul and the hungry soul He fills with good things. Psalm 107:8-9

Cultivate a grateful heart: To give thanks to the Lord, we must have a grateful heart. Gratitude is a mindset and an attitude that we can develop through daily practices such as journaling, meditation, prayer, and acts of kindness. When we focus on the good in our lives, we are better able to recognize and appreciate the blessings that the Lord has bestowed upon us.

Thank God for specific blessings: When we pray, we can thank God for specific blessings in our lives. We can thank Him for our health, our family, our friends, our job, our home, and any other blessings that we have received. When we thank God for specific blessings, we show our appreciation for His provision and grace.

Express gratitude in your actions: Giving thanks to the Lord is not just about saying "thank you." It's also about living out that gratitude in our actions. We can show our gratitude by serving others, being kind, and sharing our blessings with those in need. When we express gratitude in our actions, we honor God and show our appreciation for the blessings He has given us. Expected and unexpected.

Remember to thank God during difficult times: It's easy to thank God when things are going well, but it's just as important to thank Him during difficult times. When we face challenges, we can thank God for His presence, His strength, and His guidance. We can also thank Him for the lessons we learn through difficult experiences.

THE WORD CHANGES EVERYTHING

In conclusion, giving thanks to the Lord is a way of acknowledging His goodness and grace in our lives. By cultivating a grateful heart, thanking God for specific blessings, expressing gratitude in our actions, and remembering to thank Him during difficult times, we can deepen our relationship with God and experience His love and blessings in new and profound ways.

Are you thanking God daily?

Do you find it hard to thank God in challenging times?

Are you focused on the good that God brings into your life?

How do you cultivate a grateful heart?

Prayer: Lord, thank You for helping me to see the importance of being thankful for all the good You are doing in my life. Thank You for Your grace and Your mercy. Help me to always keep my eyes on You and not my circumstances.

CHAPTER 20

THE WORD CHANGES EVERYTHING

I HAVE BEEN BROUGHT WITH A PRICE

THE WORD CHANGES EVERYTHING

> Do you not know that your body is temple of the Holy Spirit Who lives within you, Whom you have received as a gift from God? You are not your own.
>
> You were brought with a price purchased with a preciousness and paid for, made His own. So then, honor God and bring glory to Him in your body. 1 Corinthians 6:19-20

The idea of being "bought with a price" comes from several passages in the Bible, including 1 Corinthians 6:19-20, which says, "Do you not know that your bodies are temples of the Holy Spirit, who is in you, whom you have received from God? You are not your own; you were bought at a price. Therefore, Do honor God with your bodies."

This passage emphasizes the idea that, as believers, we belong to God and are called to honor Him with our bodies, which includes taking care of ourselves physically and spiritually. This concept is also related to the idea of stewardship, which is the idea that we are responsible for taking care of the resources that God has given us, including our time, talents, and possessions.

The price that was paid for our redemption was the sacrifice of Jesus Christ on the cross. Through his death and resurrection, Jesus provided a way for us to be reconciled to God and to have eternal life. This sacrifice demonstrates the depth of God's love for us and the lengths He was willing to go to redeem us.

As a result of being "bought with a price," we are called to live our lives in a way that reflects this reality. This means seeking to honor God in all that we do and recognizing that our lives are not our own but rather belong to God. We are called to use our time, talents, and resources in a way that brings glory to God and furthers His purposes in the world.

In summary, the concept of being "bought with a price" is a reminder of the depth of God's love for us and the sacrifice that was made on our behalf. It is a call to live a life that reflects this reality and to use our lives in a way that honors God and furthers His purposes in the world.

THE WORD CHANGES EVERYTHING

Do you realize that you were brought with a price?

How are you taking care of your body?

What does 1 Corinthians 6:19-20 mean to you?

Do you realize that we belong to God and are called to honor Him with our bodies, which includes taking care of ourselves physically and spiritually?

> **Prayer:** Lord, thank You for showing me that my body is a temple holy and acceptable unto You. Lord, please help me to treat my body with honor. Lord, I am grateful for the ultimate sacrifice You made for me.

CHAPTER 21

THE WORD CHANGES EVERYTHING

I HAVE THE POWER TO CREATE WEALTH

> But thou shalt remember the Lord thy God: for it is he that giveth thee the power to get wealth, that He may establish His covenant which He swore unto thy father as it is this day. Deuteronomy 8:18

Creating wealth is the process of building financial assets and resources over time. It can provide individuals and communities with a wide range of benefits, including greater financial stability, improved quality of life, and increased opportunities for growth and success. Remember this that your power to create wealth comes from the Lord.

Income and Expenses: One of the fundamental principles of wealth creation is the need to increase income and reduce expenses. Increasing income can be achieved by improving skills, acquiring education, starting a business, or investing in financial markets. Reducing expenses, on the other hand, requires discipline and smart money management. By controlling expenses, individuals can free up resources to save and invest in the future.

Savings and Investment: Saving and investing are crucial components of wealth creation. Saving involves setting aside a portion of your income regularly, while investing involves putting your money to work to generate returns. Both can help to grow wealth over time.

Compound Interest: Compound interest is a powerful tool that can help individuals to build wealth over the long term. It involves earning interest not only on the principal amount invested but also on the accumulated interest earned over time. By reinvesting your returns, your wealth can grow exponentially.

Diversification: Diversification involves spreading your investments across different asset classes to minimize risk. This can include stocks, bonds, real estate, and other types of investments. By diversifying your portfolio, you can reduce the risk of losing money in any one area and potentially increase returns.

Patience and Discipline: Wealth creation is a long-term process that requires patience and discipline. Success is not achieved overnight but rather through consistent effort and smart decision-making over time. Staying focused on your goals and avoiding short-term temptations can help you achieve greater success in the long run.

In conclusion, creating wealth is a powerful tool that can help individuals and communities to achieve greater financial stability, increased opportunities for growth and success, and improved quality of life. By focusing on income and expenses, savings and investment, compound interest, diversification, patience, and discipline, individuals can build the financial resources they need to achieve their goals and dreams.

THE WORD CHANGES EVERYTHING

Are you challenged with saving?

Are you willing to start saving?

Are you willing to learn more about investing?

Is there anything that scares you about investing?

> **Prayer:** Thank You, Lord, for giving me the power to create wealth. Thank You for showing me how to walk in the power You have given me. Thank You for the many blessings You have given me to be a blessing not only to myself but to others.

CHAPTER 22

THE WORD CHANGES EVERYTHING

I HEAR YOU LORD

THE WORD CHANGES EVERYTHING

So, then faith cometh by hearing, and hearing by the word of God
Romans 10:17

The word of God can provide guidance, comfort, and a sense of purpose to those who seek it.

Cultivate a receptive heart: The first step in hearing the word of God is to be open and receptive to it. Be willing to listen, reflect, and act on what you hear. Cultivate a humble, teachable spirit and approach the word of God with an open mind and heart.

Engage in regular study and prayer: Hearing the word of God requires ongoing effort and engagement. Make time each day to study scripture and pray for understanding and guidance. As you deepen your understanding of God's word, you will become better equipped to hear and respond to it.

Seek guidance from trusted Godly mentors and teachers: Surround yourself with people who can help you interpret and apply the word of God in your life. Seek out trusted mentors, pastors, or teachers who can provide insight, guidance, and accountability.

Act on what you hear: Hearing the word of God is not just about intellectual understanding; it is also about taking action. When you hear something that resonates with you, take steps to incorporate it into your life. This may involve making changes to your behavior, attitudes, or relationships.

Stay humble and open to correction: Hearing the word of God is an ongoing process that requires humility and openness to correction.

THE WORD CHANGES EVERYTHING

Recognize that you are fallible and that you may need to make adjustments as you grow in your understanding of God's word.

By cultivating a receptive heart, engaging in regular study and prayer, seeking guidance from trusted mentors, acting on what you hear, and staying humble and open to correction, you can deepen your relationship with God and hear his word more clearly in your life.

Are you open to taking Godly Correction?

How open are you to acting on what you hear from God?

Do you seek Godly wisdom?

Is your heart receptive to the word of God?

> **Prayer:** Lord, help me to keep my mind and heart open to hearing You when You speak to me. Help me keep my focus on You, always knowing that You have my best interest at heart.

CHAPTER 23

THE WORD CHANGES EVERYTHING

I KNOW THE VOICE OF GOD

THE WORD CHANGES EVERYTHING

> The sheep that are my own hear and are listening to My voice; and I know them, and they follow Me. John 10:27

Many believe that God speaks to them through a still, small voice, often called a "whisper." This voice is said to be gentle, loving, and peaceful and may provide guidance, comfort, or wisdom. I believe this is the voice of the Holy Spirit.

Hearing the voice of God is important to develop a personal relationship with Him. You can do this through prayer, meditation, and studying His word. By doing so, you can cultivate a deep sense of discernment and clarity that can help you recognize God's voice amidst the noise and chaos of daily life.

It is also essential to stay open-minded and receptive to hearing God's voice, even if it doesn't come in the way you expect or desire. God may speak to you through other people, circumstances, or even unexpected events in your life.

However, it is important to note that discerning the voice of God is a deeply personal and subjective experience, and what may be true for one person may not necessarily be true for another. Therefore, it is important to approach this topic with an open mind and heart and to seek guidance and wisdom from trusted spiritual leaders or mentors if you have any questions or doubts.

THE WORD CHANGES EVERYTHING

Do you know the voice of God?

When God speaks to you, do you always pay attention?

It is also essential to stay open-minded and receptive to hearing God's voice, even if it doesn't come in the way you expect or desire. What are your thoughts?

God may speak to you through other people, circumstances, or even unexpected events in your life. What are your thoughts?

> **Prayer:** Lord, thank You for allowing me to hear Your voice. Thank You for showing me that Your great voice guides me in all areas of my life. Thank You for Your wisdom, power, kindness, and love.

CHAPTER 24

THE WORD CHANGES EVERYTHING

I MUST ASK

THE WORD CHANGES EVERYTHING

> In that day you will ask nothing of me. Truly, truly, I say to you, whatever you ask of the Father in my name, He will give it to you. Until now you have asked nothing in my name. Ask, and you will receive, that your joy may be full. John 16: 23-24

Throughout history, people have turned to prayer to communicate with God and express their desires, hopes, and fears. There are benefits to asking God for what we want in life. And it is important to line our desires with the will of God.

Firstly, asking God for what we want can help us clarify our desires and priorities. When we take the time to reflect on what we truly want, we are more likely to identify what truly matters to us. By articulating our desires to God, we can gain clarity and focus on our goals. Psalms 32:8 tell us that God will instruct us and show us the way to go. He will watch over us and guide us with His eyes.

Secondly, asking God for what we want can help us cultivate a sense of gratitude and trust. When we believe that God is listening to us and cares about our desires, we may feel more grateful for the blessings in our lives. Additionally, we may develop a sense of trust that God will provide for us in the way that is best for us, even if it is not exactly what we asked for.

Finally, asking God for what we want can help us feel more connected to a higher purpose or meaning. When we believe that there is a divine plan for our lives, we may feel more motivated and inspired to pursue our goals. We may also feel more comforted and supported during difficult times, knowing that God is with us and we are not alone in our struggles.

Overall, asking God for what we want can have a positive impact on our lives. Whether we are seeking material possessions, spiritual growth, or emotional healing, prayer can be a powerful tool for transformation and self-discovery. However, it is important to remember that prayer is not a substitute for action. We must also take responsibility for our own lives and work towards our goals with determination and persistence.

Are you intentional about asking God for what you want?

Are you comfortable about asking God for what you want?

Do you believe asking God for what you want will have a positive impact on your life?

How does it make you feel about seeking God for what you want?

Prayer: Lord, thank You for allowing me to come to You freely for the desires of my heart. Thank You for being a God that answers the prayers of Your people.

CHAPTER 25

THE WORD CHANGES EVERYTHING

I SHALL SEEK MY GOD AT ALL TIMES

THE WORD CHANGES EVERYTHING

> But seek first the kingdom of God and His righteousness and all these things will be added to you Therefore don't worry about tomorrow for tomorrow will take care of itself. Matthew 6:33-34

Seeking God at all times is essential to a fulfilling spiritual life. It means making a conscious effort to connect with God in everything you do every day. Here are some critical points on seeking God at all times:

Make time for prayer: A prayer is a crucial tool for seeking God's presence. It allows you to express gratitude, ask for guidance, and share your concerns. Set aside a specific time each day for prayer and make it a habit.

Stay mindful: Be mindful of God's presence throughout your day. Try to stay present and focused on your spiritual journey and look for ways to connect with God in your daily activities.

Read the Bible: The Bible is an excellent source of guidance and inspiration. It is our Manuel for life. Take time to read it regularly and seek wisdom from its teachings.

Surround yourself with people of faith: Seek out others who share your desire to seek God. Join a church, attend Bible studies or prayer groups, and connect with like-minded individuals who can support and encourage you on your spiritual journey.

Practice gratitude: Expressing gratitude is a powerful way to seek God's presence. Take time each day to reflect on the blessings in your life and thank God for them.

Trust in God's plan: Seeking God also means trusting in His plan for your life. Surrender your worries and fears to Him and have faith that He will guide you on the right path.

Be open to God's presence: God is present in all things, but it's up to us to be open to His presence. Stay open to the signs and messages He sends you and be willing to follow where He leads.

In conclusion, seeking God at all times is a lifelong journey that requires dedication, mindfulness, and faith. By praying, reading the Bible, surrounding yourself with people who choose to walk in faith, practicing gratitude, trusting in God's plan, and staying open to His presence, you can deepen your spiritual connection and experience the fullness of God's love in your life.

THE WORD CHANGES EVERYTHING

Are you seeking God in times of need?

How hard is it for you to trust the plans of God?

What do you do when you are not operating in the spirit of gratitude?

Are you surrounding yourself with people of faith?

> **Prayer:** Lord, thank You for showing me the importance of seeking You first. Thank you for being so willing to shed light on my life continuously. Thank You for showing me the importance of trusting your plans for my life.

CHAPTER 26

THE WORD CHANGES EVERYTHING

I SPEAK GREAT WORDS FROM MY HEART

THE WORD CHANGES EVERYTHING

For out of the heart the mouth speaks. The good person out of Her good treasure brings forth good. Matthew 12:34-35

Speaking great words from your heart requires practice and intention. It is essential to talk about the word of God. When we do that, great things come forth.

Know your audience: Before you speak, consider who you are talking to and what they are interested in hearing. Tailor your message to resonate with them.

Be authentic: Be true to yourself when you speak from the heart. Don't try to be someone else or say things you don't believe in.

Use emotion: Emotion is a powerful tool in communication. Use it to connect with your audience and convey your message in a compelling way.

Tell stories: Stories are a great way to capture people's attention and convey your message. Use personal stories or anecdotes to illustrate your point and make it more memorable.

Practice, practice, practice: Speaking from the heart is a skill that can be improved with practice. Take every opportunity to speak publicly or in front of friends and family to increase your skills.

Be concise: Great words from the heart are often simple and to the point. Avoid rambling or using unnecessary jargon that may confuse your audience.

THE WORD CHANGES EVERYTHING

Believe in yourself: Have confidence in speaking from the heart. Trust that your message is essential, and you have something valuable to say.

Remember, speaking from the heart is not just about your words but also how you say them. Be confident, authentic, and emotionally connected to your message, and your comments will impact your audience.

Do you find it hard to speak from your heart?

Do you believe in your power to transform the lives of others?

How do you feel about telling your story?

Do you feel like you are authentic?

> **Prayer:** Lord, teach me to speak from my heart. Lord, Thank You for helping me keep control of my emotions. Help me to be the authentic person You have called me to be.

CHAPTER 27

THE WORD CHANGES EVERYTHING

I AM WALKING IN THE CONFIDENCE OF THE LORD

> Let us then, with confidence, draw near to the throne of grace, that we may receive mercy and find grace to help in time of need. Hebrews 4:16

Walking in the confidence of Christ can be a transformative experience that can change the way we approach life, interact with others, and handle challenges. Here are some key lessons on how to walk in the confidence of Christ:

Know who you are in Christ: When walking in the confidence of Christ, it's essential to understand your identity as a child of God. You are loved, accepted, and forgiven, and nothing can change that. When you have a deep understanding of your worth in Christ, you can approach life with a newfound confidence that comes from knowing that you are loved by God.

Focus on God's promises: The Bible is full of promises that God has made to His children. When you focus on these promises, you can trust that God will fulfill them in your life. Whether it's a promise of protection, provision, or guidance, knowing that God is faithful to His promises can give you the confidence to face any challenge that comes your way.

Surrender your fears to God: Fear is a common obstacle that can prevent us from walking in the confidence of Christ. However, when we surrender our fears to God and trust Him to guide us, we can overcome any fear and approach life with boldness and confidence.

Seek wisdom and guidance from God: When we face challenges or difficult decisions, it's essential to seek wisdom and guidance from God. Through prayer, reading the Bible, and seeking the counsel of other believers, we can gain the clarity we need to make wise decisions and approach life with confidence.

Practice gratitude: Gratitude is a powerful way to cultivate confidence and joy in your life. When you focus on the blessings and goodness of God, you can approach life with a positive mindset and a heart full of gratitude. This can help you to overcome any negative thoughts or emotions that might be holding you back and walk in the confidence of Christ.

In conclusion, walking in the confidence of Christ is a journey that requires intentionality, faith, and trust in God. By focusing on your identity in Christ, trusting in His promises, surrendering your fears to Him, seeking wisdom and guidance, and cultivating gratitude, you can approach life with the boldness and confidence that comes from knowing that God is with you every step of the way.

THE WORD CHANGES EVERYTHING

Are you seeking the guidance of the Lord?

Are you confident in who you are in Christ?

Are focused on the promise of God?

How willing are you to surrender all your concerns to God?

> **Prayer:** Lord, thank You for allowing me a place where I can bring all my concerns to You. Thank You for showing me that fear has no place in my life and that I must continue to embrace faith as I follow my destiny.

CHAPTER 28

THE WORD CHANGES EVERYTHING

I WILL EXHORT THE LORD ALWAYS

THE WORD CHANGES EVERYTHING

> Rejoice In the Lord always delight, gladden yourselves in Him; again, I say, Rejoice. Philippians 4:4

Exhorting the Lord always is an important aspect of the Christian faith. It involves continually praising and worshiping God, expressing gratitude, seeking guidance, and making requests through prayer. In this lesson, we will explore the meaning and significance of exhorting the Lord always.

Exhorting the Lord always means calling upon God and making requests, expressing gratitude, and seeking guidance from Him at all times. It is a way of acknowledging God's sovereignty and submitting to His will. The Bible encourages believers to exhort the Lord always in several passages, including Philippians 4:6-7, which says, "Do not be anxious about anything, but in everything by prayer and supplication with thanksgiving let your requests be made known to God. And the peace of God, which surpasses all understanding, will guard your hearts and your minds in Christ Jesus."

Exhorting the Lord always is an act of faith that demonstrates our trust in God's ability to provide for our needs and guide us through life's challenges. It also strengthens our relationship with God as we learn to rely on Him for everything. Through prayer and exhortation, we invite God to be present in our lives and to work in us and through us.

Moreover, exhorting the Lord always is not only about making requests and expressing gratitude but also about worshiping God. When we exhort the Lord, we acknowledge His greatness, goodness, and power. When we praise Him for who He is and for what He has done. We declare our love and devotion to Him, and we offer Him our lives as a living sacrifice.

THE WORD CHANGES EVERYTHING

In conclusion, exhorting the Lord always is an essential part of the Christian life. It is a way of staying connected to God and growing in our faith. It involves making requests, expressing gratitude, seeking guidance, and worshiping God through prayer. As we exhort the Lord, we demonstrate our trust in God, and we invite Him to work in us and through us for His glory.

Where are you with your relationship with the Lord?

How important is God's sovereignty to you?

What do you do when you are anxious?

How much do you trust God with your circumstances?

> **Prayer:** Lord, thank You for helping me see how important it is to trust You in all circumstances. Thank You for showing me the importance of Exhorting You at all times.

CHAPTER 29

THE WORD CHANGES EVERYTHING

I WILL GIVE MY TROUBLES TO THE LORD

THE WORD CHANGES EVERYTHING

Cast your care upon the Lord for He cares for you. 1 Peter 5:7

I want to add if we surrender our cares to the Lord, He will in fact take of them.

Acknowledge your troubles: The first step in giving your problems to the Lord is to acknowledge what is troubling you. It could be a difficult situation, a problem that you cannot solve, or a feeling that is overwhelming you. Take some time to reflect on what is causing you distress. And then turn them over to the Lord.

Pray: A prayer is a powerful tool that you can use to give your troubles to the Lord. You can pray to God, Jesus, and the Holy Spirit, Ask for guidance, strength, and comfort. Pour out your heart to God and ask Him to take care of your troubles.

Trust in the Lord: Once you have prayed, it's important to trust that the Lord has heard your prayers and will answer them in His time. It can be difficult to wait, especially when you are going through a tough time, but trust that the Lord has a plan for your life and that He will guide you through your troubles.

Seek support: While waiting for the Lord to answer your prayers, seek support from your family, friends, or a professional counselor. Talking about your troubles can help you process your emotions and gain new perspectives.

Practice gratitude: Even in the midst of difficult circumstances, it's important to practice gratitude. Take some time to reflect on the good things in your life, such as your health, family, friends, and faith.

THE WORD CHANGES EVERYTHING

Focusing on the positive can help you feel more hopeful and optimistic about the future.

Remember that giving your troubles to the Lord is a continuous process. It's not a one-time event but a daily practice. You may have to give your troubles to the Lord many times throughout your life but know that He is always there to guide you through your struggles.

What does the scripture mean to you? (1 Peter 5:7)

How do you focus on the positive in the challenging times in your life?

Once you have prayed about your problem, do leave it in the hands of God.

What are you most grateful for from God?

> **Prayer:** Lord, thank You for all Your many blessings. Thank You for not giving up on me. Thank You for seeing in me that which I didn't see in myself. There is no greater love than the love You have for me.

CHAPTER 30

THE WORD CHANGES EVERYTHING

I WILL HUMBLE MYSELF BEFORE THE LORD

> Therefore, humble yourselves, lower yourselves in your own estimation under the mighty hand of God, that in due time He may exalt you.
> 1 Peter 5:6

Humbling oneself before the Lord is an important aspect of spiritual growth and maturity. It involves recognizing our own limitations and weaknesses in the presence of God and acknowledging His sovereignty and greatness.

Recognize God's sovereignty: Humility begins with recognizing that God is the Creator and Sustainer of all things and that He is in control of our lives. This means acknowledging that our own abilities and accomplishments are ultimately dependent on God's grace and mercy.

Confess our sinfulness: Humility also involves acknowledging our own sinfulness and need for forgiveness. This means being honest with ourselves and God about our mistakes, weaknesses, and failures and seeking His mercy and grace to overcome them.

Submit to God's will: Humility involves surrendering our own desires and plans to God's will for our lives. This means trusting that He knows what is best for us, even if it may be different from what we had planned or hoped for.

Serve others: Humility also involves putting the needs of others before our own. This means seeking opportunities to serve and help others and recognizing that our own talents and resources are gifts from God to be used for His purposes.

Practice gratitude: Humility involves cultivating a spirit of gratitude and thankfulness for all that God has given us. This means recognizing that everything we have is a gift from Him and expressing our gratitude through prayer and acts of kindness to others.

In conclusion, humbling oneself before the Lord involves recognizing God's sovereignty, confessing our sinfulness, submitting to God's will, serving others, and practicing gratitude. By embracing these lessons, we can grow in our relationship with God and experience the peace and joy that comes from living a humble and obedient life.

THE WORD CHANGES EVERYTHING

Share how you believe that God is sovereign in your life.

How do you practice gratitude in your life?

How do you serve others?

Are you honest about your mistakes in your life?

> **Prayer:** Lord, thank You for allowing me Your Grace and Mercy. Thank You for Your sovereignty. Thank You for acts of kindness towards me. Thank You for helping me to always see the importance of turning to You.

CHAPTER 31

THE WORD CHANGES EVERYTHING

I WILL PRAISE HIM AT ALL TIMES

But a woman that fears Jehovah, she shall be praised. Give her of the fruit of her hands; And let her works praise her in the gates. Proverbs 31:30-31

Understanding the Phrase:
A. Praise: Praise refers to expressing admiration, gratitude, and worship to God. It involves acknowledging God's greatness, goodness, and faithfulness.
B. "At all times": This phrase emphasizes that our praise to the Lord should not be limited to specific moments or circumstances. It calls for a continuous attitude of praise, regardless of our situations.

Biblical Basis:
Psalm 34:1-3: The inspiration for this scripture can be found in Psalm 34:1, which says, "I will bless the Lord at all times; his praise shall continually be in my mouth." The psalmist expresses a determined commitment to praise God continually, regardless of the circumstances.

Psalm 145:2: Another verse that supports this scripture is Psalm 145:2, which says, "Every day I will bless you and praise your name forever and ever." Here, the psalmist emphasizes the daily nature of praising God.

Reasons for Praising the Lord at All Times:
God's Unchanging Nature: God remains constant and faithful, irrespective of our circumstances. We can find confidence and strength in praising Him, knowing that He is always with us.

Gratitude and Contentment: Praising God at all times cultivates a grateful heart, helping us focus on His blessings and provision, even in challenging times.

Declaring God's Greatness: Praising the Lord publicly and consistently allows us to testify to His greatness and serve as a witness to others.

Benefits of Praising God at All Times:
Spiritual Nourishment: Continuous praise deepens our connection with God, leading us to spiritual growth and a closer relationship with Him.

Joy and Encouragement: Praise uplifts our spirits, brings joy to our hearts, and strengthens us during difficult seasons.

Victorious Perspective: Praising God helps shift our focus from our problems to His power, reminding us of His sovereignty and enabling us to face challenges with confidence.

Practical Application: Cultivate a Habit of Praise: Incorporate praise and worship into your daily routine, making it a natural part of your life.

Choose Gratitude: Develop an attitude of gratitude by intentionally focusing on God's blessings and expressing thankfulness.

Share Your Testimony: Sharing your experiences of God's faithfulness and goodness with others will help and encourage non-believers and fellow believers of the goodness of God.

Conclusion:
Praising the Lord at all times is not just a phrase; it is a transformative way of life. By embracing continuous praise, we can experience the joy, strength, and blessings that come from a deep relationship with God. May we strive to cultivate a heart of praise, glorifying God in all circumstances.

THE WORD CHANGES EVERYTHING

How do you feel when you are praising God?

Do you feel like you have a heart of gratitude?

What do you do for spiritual nourishment?

How do you encourage yourself when you feel like you are off course?

Prayer: Lord, thank You for showing me the importance of always praising You. Thank You for encouraging me in my time of need and showing me when the prayers go up, the blessings come flowing down.

CHAPTER 32

THE WORD CHANGES EVERYTHING

I WILL SEEK THE LORD AT ALL TIMES

> Ask and it will be given to you; seek and you will find; knock and the door will be open to you. For everyone who asks receives; he who seeks finds; and to him who knocks the door will be open. Matthew 7:7-8

Seeking the Lord for everything means making Him the center of your life and relying on Him for guidance, strength, and provision in every aspect of your life. Here are some important points to consider:

Trust in the Lord's sovereignty: Seeking the Lord means acknowledging His sovereignty and submitting to His will. Trusting that He has a plan and purpose for your life and that He is in control will help you find peace and security in the midst of life's challenges.

Pray regularly: Prayer is an essential part of seeking the Lord. It is how we communicate with Him, and it allows us to bring our worries, fears, and concerns to Him. Make a habit of setting aside time each day to pray and be honest and open with God about your struggles and desires.

Read and study the Bible: The Bible is God's word, and it contains everything we need to know about who God is and how we should live. Regularly reading and studying the Bible will help you grow in your understanding of God and His will for your life.

Seek wise counsel: Seeking the Lord doesn't mean you have to do everything alone. God has placed wise and experienced people in your life to help guide and mentor you. Seek out godly counsel from people you trust and be open to their advice and wisdom.

Obey God's commands: Seeking the Lord means following His commands and living according to His will. This may require making difficult choices and sacrifices, but it is essential for living a life that honors and pleases God.

Give thanks in all circumstances: Seeking the Lord means being grateful for all that He has given you, even in difficult circumstances. Remember that God is faithful, and He will provide for your needs as you seek Him.

In summary, seeking the Lord for everything requires faith, obedience, and a commitment to live according to His will. It is a lifelong journey that requires constant effort and reliance on God's strength and wisdom. But as you seek the Lord, He will guide you and provide for you, and you will find true joy and fulfillment in Him.

THE WORD CHANGES EVERYTHING

How often do you study the word of God?

Do you find it hard to give thanks in the midst of your circumstances?

Do you find it hard to obey God's commands?

How do you go about seeking God's council?

> **Prayer:** Lord, help me to always seek You. Help me to never forget the price You paid for me on calvary.

CHAPTER 33

THE WORD CHANGES EVERYTHING

I WILL SING PRAISES TO MY GOD

O Come, let us sing to the Lord; let us make a joyful noise to the Rock of our salvation! Let us come before His presence with thanksgiving; let us make a joyful noise to Him with songs of praise. For the Lord is a great God and a great King above all gods. Psalm 95:1-3

"I will sing praises to my Lord" is a statement of faith and commitment to worship God through song. Singing praises to God is an act of worship that has been a part of Christian traditions for centuries.

Praise is an important aspect of worship: Praising God is a way of acknowledging His greatness, His goodness, and His power. When we sing praises to God, we are expressing our gratitude and adoration for who He is and what He has done for us. As such, praising God should be an integral part of our worship.

Worship is a personal choice: The statement "I will sing praises to my Lord" emphasizes the personal choice to worship God. We must each make the decision to worship God, acknowledge His sovereignty over our lives, and express our devotion to Him through song.

Worship can be joyful: Singing praises to God can be a joyful experience. When we sing praises to God, we are expressing our joy and happiness in Him. It is an opportunity to celebrate the goodness of God and to express our gratitude for all He has done for us.

Worship can be a form of spiritual warfare: Singing praises to God can also be a form of spiritual warfare. When we sing praises to God, we declare His power and authority over all things. This can be a powerful tool in the fight against the spiritual forces of darkness.

THE WORD CHANGES EVERYTHING

In summary, the statement "I will sing praises to my Lord" reminds us of the importance of praising God, the personal choice to worship Him, the joy of worship, and the power of worship as a form of spiritual warfare.

Did you realize that singing praise to God is a sword against the enemy?

Did you realize that singing praises to God will bring joy to your heart?

Why do you think that worship is a personal choice that God has given us?

How has worshiping and praising God helped you in tough times?

> **Prayer:** Lord, thank You for showing me the importance of worshiping and praising You. Thank You for always giving me Your love and kindness.

CHAPTER 34

THE WORD CHANGES EVERYTHING

I WILL TRUST IN THE LORD

THE WORD CHANGES EVERYTHING

> Trust In the Lord with all your heart and do not lean on your understanding . In all your ways acknowledge Him, and He will make your pathway straight. Proverbs 3:5-6

Trusting in the Lord is a central aspect of our Christian belief and can provide comfort and guidance during times of difficulty. Here are some key points on trusting in the Lord:

Have faith: Trusting in the Lord requires faith, which means believing in something without necessarily having proof. Faith is considered a gift from God that can be strengthened through prayer and worship.

Surrender control: Trusting in the Lord also requires surrendering control. It means acknowledging that you are not in charge of everything and that there are certain things that are beyond your control. By surrendering control, you allow God to guide your life and help you through difficult times so that, eventually, you will be able to see the possibilities God has to offer you.

Seek guidance: One way to trust in the Lord is to seek guidance through prayer and scripture, and Godly advice. As Christians, we are encouraged to pray regularly and to read The word of God for guidance and inspiration.

Be patient: Trusting in the Lord often requires patience. Sometimes, it may seem like God is not answering your prayers or that things are not going the way you want them to. However, it's important to remember that God works in miraculous ways and that everything happens for a reason.

Lean on others: Finally, it's important to lean on others for support when you are struggling to trust in the Lord. This could mean seeking out a spiritual mentor, talking to friends and family members who share your beliefs.

Remember, trusting in the Lord is a journey that requires patience, faith, and surrender. By seeking guidance, being patient, and leaning on others for support, you can deepen your trust in God and find peace and comfort in difficult times.

THE WORD CHANGES EVERYTHING

Has trusting God been easy for you or hard?

Do you lean on others when you are struggling to trust God?

How do you surrender yourself to God?

Is it hard for you to have faith when you are going through life's challenges?

> **Prayer:** Lord, thank You for teaching me how to trust You through the good times and the bad times. Thank You for showing me those to lean on when I am not willing to trust. Most importantly, Thank You for showing me how to surrender myself to Your will.

CHAPTER 35

THE WORD CHANGES EVERYTHING

I WILL WAIT PATIENTLY ON THE LORD

THE WORD CHANGES EVERYTHING

Be still before the Lord and wait patiently for Him; Psalm 37:7

Waiting patiently for the Lord is an essential part of the Christian faith. It is a reminder that God is in control and that we need to trust in His timing and plan for our lives.

Trust in God's plan: Waiting on the Lord requires a deep trust in His plan for your life. Sometimes, God's plan may not make sense to us, but we must believe that He knows what is best for us. As it says in Proverbs 3:5-6, "Trust in the Lord with all your heart and lean not on your own understanding; in all your ways submit to him, and he will make your paths straight."

Be still and wait: Waiting patiently for the Lord also means being still and waiting. We live in a fast-paced world where we want everything now, but God's timing is different from ours. Psalm 46:10 says, "Be still, and know that I am God." This verse reminds us to slow down and be patient, knowing that God is in control.

Pray and seek God's guidance: While waiting on the Lord, we should be praying and seeking His guidance. Philippians 4:6, it says, "Do not be anxious about anything, but in every situation, by prayer and petition, with thanksgiving, present your requests to God." We should be in constant communication with God, asking for His wisdom and guidance.

Use the time wisely: Waiting on the Lord can be a time of preparation. Use this time to draw closer to God, to study His word, and to serve others. Galatians 6:9 says, "Let us not become weary in doing good, for at the proper time we will reap a harvest if we do not give up." Keep doing good, even in the waiting.

Remember God's faithfulness: Finally, while waiting patiently for the Lord, remember His faithfulness. Look back at how God has worked in your life in the past and trust that He will continue to work in the future. In Psalm 27:14, it says, "Wait for the Lord; be strong and take heart and wait for the Lord."

In conclusion, waiting patiently for the Lord requires trust, stillness, prayer, the wise use of time, and remembering His faithfulness. May we all learn to wait patiently for the Lord and trust in His perfect timing and plan for our lives.

THE WORD CHANGES EVERYTHING

Waiting on the Lord requires a deep trust in His plan for your life. What are your thoughts?

Waiting patiently for the Lord also means being still and waiting. What are your thoughts?

While waiting on the Lord, we should be praying and seeking His guidance. What are your thoughts?

Waiting on the Lord can be a time of preparation. Use this time to draw closer to God, to study His word, and to serve others. What are your thoughts?

Prayer: Lord, thank You for showing me the importance of being still and waiting on You. Thank You for showing me how to use my time wisely.

CHAPTER 36

THE WORD CHANGES EVERYTHING

LORD HELP ME FIGHT THE GOOD FIGHT

> I have fought the good worthy, honorable, and noble fight, I have finished the race, I have kept (firmly held) the faith. 2 Timothy 4:7

"Lord, help me fight the good fight" is commonly used in Christian circles, particularly during moments of difficulty and challenge. The phrase is based on a passage from the Bible, 2 Timothy 4:7, which reads, "I have fought the good fight, I have finished the race, I have kept the faith." This passage is often interpreted to mean that believers should persevere in their faith despite any difficulties they may encounter. Here are some key points that we can draw from this phrase:

Recognize that life is a battle: The phrase "fight the good fight" implies that in life, we will encounter struggles and that there will be times when we will face obstacles and challenges. But it is important to recognize this reality and prepare ourselves mentally, emotionally, and spiritually for the battles that we may face and know that God will help us face these battles.

Keep the faith: Another key lesson we can all learn is to stay committed to our beliefs and values, even when it's difficult. This means trusting in God's plan, even when we don't understand it, and relying on His strength and guidance to help us persevere.

Stay focused on the goal: In 2 Timothy 4:7, the writer talks about "finishing the race." This suggests that we should stay focused on our ultimate goal, which is to live a life that is pleasing to God. This can help us stay motivated during difficult times and can give us a sense of purpose and direction in our lives.

Lean on others for support: Finally, it's important to recognize that we don't have to fight the battle alone. We can lean on our family, friends, and community for support, as well as on God, through prayer and reading the word of God.

In summary, "Lord, help me fight the good fight" is a powerful phrase that reminds us of the challenges we may face in life and encourages us to stay committed to our faith and values. By keeping these lessons in mind, we can find strength and courage in difficult times and continue to pursue the life that God has called us to live.

THE WORD CHANGES EVERYTHING

Do you feel like you are in a battle right now? Know you are not alone!

Fighting the good fight" implies that life is a struggle and that there will be times when we will face obstacles and challenges. But know that Christ has come to overcome them for you. What are your thoughts?

Another key lesson is to stay committed to our beliefs, faith, and values, even when it's difficult. What are your thoughts?

In 2 Timothy 4:7, The writer talks about "finishing the race." This suggests that we should stay focused on our dreams and our goals and never give up. What are your thoughts?

> **Prayer:** Lord, thank You for showing us the importance of not giving up on what You have placed in our hearts. Thank You for showing us that we can accomplish anything we desire because You promised that You would give us the desires of our hearts.

CHAPTER 37
THE WORD CHANGES EVERYTHING

LORD LEAD ME TO YOUR TRUTH

> Make me to know your ways, O Lord; teach me your paths. Lead me in your truth and teach me, for you are the God of my salvation; for you I wait all day long Psalm 25:4-5

God and His truth is a deeply personal and subjective topic that can be approached from many different perspectives. However, there are a few key concepts and principles that are commonly associated with the search for God's truth.

Faith: Faith is a belief in something that cannot be proven through natural evidence. It is a deeply personal conviction that can be based on supernatural evidence, personal experiences, or a combination of both. To discover God's truth, one must have faith in His existence and His teachings.

Prayer and meditation: Prayer and meditation are practices that we as Christians, use to connect with God and seek His guidance. These practices can help individuals develop a deeper understanding of God's will and help them discern His truth.

Studying the word of God: Contains teachings and stories that can help individuals understand God's truth. By studying God's word and reflecting on its meaning, one can gain a deeper understanding of God's will.

Seeking guidance from spiritual leaders: Spiritual leaders, such as pastors and other spiritual leaders, can offer guidance and support in one's search for God's truth. They may be able to offer insights and interpretations of the word of God that can help individuals understand God's will.

Living a moral and ethical life: Living a moral and ethical life is an important aspect of discovering God's truth. By living according to His teachings, one can develop a deeper relationship with God and gain a better understanding of His will.

In conclusion, the search for God's truth is a personal and subjective journey that can be approached in many different ways. However, by having faith, praying, meditating, studying God's word, seeking guidance from spiritual leaders, and living a moral and ethical life, one can develop a deeper understanding of who God is and His truth.

THE WORD CHANGES EVERYTHING

How often do you study God's word?

Do you walk by faith?

Do you feel you are living a moral and ethical life?

Are you comfortable seeking Godly advice?

Prayer: Lord, help me to walk by faith and not sight. Helping me to seek Godly advice. Thank You for allowing me to trust You and Your word.

CHAPTER 38

THE WORD CHANGES EVERYTHING

LOVE COVERS EVERYTHING

THE WORD CHANGES EVERYTHING

Love is patient love is kind. It does not envy, it does not boast, it is not proud. It is not rude, it is not self-seeking, it is not easily angered, it keeps no record of wrongs. Love does not delight in evil but rejoices with the truth. It always protects, always trusts, always hopes always preserves. Love never fails. 1 Corinthians 13:4

This famous passage from the Bible is often quoted at weddings and is a beautiful lesson on love. Let's break it down further to understand what it means.

Firstly, love is patient. This means that love is willing to wait and endure difficult times. It does not become impatient or frustrated easily.

Secondly, love is kind. This means that love is gentle and compassionate towards others. It seeks to help and care for them.

Thirdly, love does not envy, boast, or become proud. It does not want what others have or seek to elevate itself above others.

Fourthly, love does not dishonor others or seek its own interests. It is not self-seeking or selfish.

Fifthly, love is not easily angered and does not keep a record of wrongs. It does not hold grudges or seek revenge.

Sixthly, love does not delight in evil but rejoices with the truth. It seeks what is right and just.

Seventhly, love always protects, trusts, hopes, and perseveres. It never gives up, even in the face of difficulties.

THE WORD CHANGES EVERYTHING

Finally, love never fails. It endures all things and continues to be a source of strength and comfort. In summary, this lesson on love teaches us that true love is patient, kind, selfless, forgiving, and enduring. It is not based on selfish desires or personal gain but rather seeks the well-being and happiness of others.

In conclusion, love truly does cover everything. It has the power to transform lives, heal wounds, conquer fears, and bring people together. When we cultivate love in our lives, we create a more positive and fulfilling existence for ourselves and those around us.

THE WORD CHANGES EVERYTHING

How patient are you?

How kind are you to others?

Have you ever shown envy toward some you loved?

Are you easily angered? And if so, how do you deal with it quickly?

> **Prayer:** Lord, thank You for not allowing me to be angry unnecessarily. Thank You for showing me what true love looks like, even when I have been wronged.

CHAPTER 39

THE WORD CHANGES EVERYTHING

LOVING CHRIST

THE WORD CHANGES EVERYTHING

We love Him because He first loved us 1 John 4:19

Here I am providing some insights on how to love Christ based on the teachings of Christianity.

Seek to know Christ: The first step in loving Christ is to know Him. This involves reading the Bible and studying His life and teachings. It also involves spending time in prayer and seeking a personal relationship with Him.

Obey His commands: Jesus said, "If you love me, you will keep my commandments" (John 14:15). This means that we should strive to live our lives in accordance with His teachings and follow His example of love and service.

Serve others: Jesus demonstrated His love for others by serving them, and we are called to do the same. We can show our love for Christ by serving those in need, both within and outside of our communities.

Practice gratitude: As Christians, we believe that everything we have comes from God, and we should be thankful for His blessings. Practicing gratitude can help us cultivate a deeper love for Christ and a greater appreciation for His goodness.

Share the Gospel: Jesus commanded His disciples to "go and make disciples of all nations" (Matthew 28:19). Sharing the good news of the Gospel is an act of love, as it offers people the opportunity to know and love Christ as well.

Overall, loving Christ involves both knowing and obeying Him, serving others, practicing gratitude, and sharing the Gospel. By doing so, we can cultivate a deeper and more meaningful relationship with Him.

The first step in loving Christ is to know Him. Do You feel like you need to build a relationship with Him? (John 14:15). This means that we should strive to live our lives in accordance with His teachings and follow His example of love and service. Are you willing to follow His example?

Jesus demonstrated His love for others by serving them, and we are called to do the same. Are you open to serving others?

Sharing the good news of the Gospel is an act of love, as it offers people the opportunity to know and love Christ as well. How important is it for you to share the Gospel?

Prayer: Lord, thank You for loving us and showing us how important it is to love one another. Thank You for showing us how to cultivate a deeper and more meaningful relationship with You.

CHAPTER 40

THE WORD CHANGES EVERYTHING

MY CIRCLE OF INFLUENCE IS KEY

> Do not be deceived: "Bad company ruins good morals." For some have no knowledge of God. I say this to your shame. 1 Corinthians 15:33

Spiritual Guidance: Godly Influence can provide us with spiritual guidance, helping us to understand our purpose in life and our relationship with God. This can help us to find meaning and direction in our lives and give us a sense of peace and fulfillment.

Moral Compass: Godly Influence can also help us to develop a strong moral compass. Through exposure to the teachings and principles of God, we can learn what is right and wrong and develop a sense of personal responsibility and accountability for our actions.

Positive Role Models: Surrounding ourselves with Godly influences can also provide us with positive role models to emulate. This can help us to develop virtues such as love, compassion, forgiveness, and humility and inspire us to be our best selves.

Support and Encouragement: Having Godly influences in our lives can also provide us with support and encouragement during difficult times. This can help us to persevere through challenges and strengthen our faith and resilience.

Accountability: Finally, having Godly influences in our lives can provide us with accountability. This means that we have people who can hold us accountable for our actions and help us to stay on the right path.

This can be especially important when we are facing temptation or struggling with difficult decisions.

THE WORD CHANGES EVERYTHING

Overall, the importance of having Godly Influence in our lives cannot be overstated. By surrounding ourselves with positive role models, seeking spiritual guidance, developing a strong moral compass, receiving support and encouragement, and being held accountable, we can deepen our faith and live a life that is aligned with God's will.

THE WORD CHANGES EVERYTHING

What does your circle of influence look like in your life?

Did you know that Godly influence can also help you to develop a strong moral compass in your life?

Do you realize that having Godly influences in our lives can also provide us with support and encouragement during challenging times?

Do you realize that having Godly influences in our lives can provide us with accountability? How would that be helpful to you?

> **Prayer:** Lord, thank You for being my circle of Influence. Thank You for allowing Your word to keep me accountable to You. Thank You for bringing Godly Spiritual people into my life.

CHAPTER 41

THE WORD CHANGES EVERYTHING

MY CONFIDENCE IS IN CHRIST JESUS

THE WORD CHANGES EVERYTHING

> For we do not have a high priest who is unable to sympathize with our weakness, but one who in every respect has been tempted as we are, yet with out sin. Let us then with confidence draw near the throne of grace that we may receive the mercy and find grace to help in time of need.
> Hebrew 4: 15-16

As Christians, confidence in Christ comes from our belief in His teachings and promises. We believe that through Christ, we have been forgiven of our sins and have eternal life. This belief can give us peace and security that can boost our confidence in various areas of our lives.

In addition, as Christians, we find comfort and guidance in prayer and reading the Bible. These practices can provide us with a sense of clarity and direction, which can help us navigate challenges and make important decisions. We can also find support and encouragement from other members of our church community.

Overall, the confidence that we as Christians find in Christ can be deeply personal and meaningful to us. It may influence how we approach challenges and opportunities in our lives and can provide us with a sense of purpose and fulfillment.

THE WORD CHANGES EVERYTHING

How are you walking out your confidence in Christ?

How is the Lord using your confidence in Him?

When there are times when you don't feel very confident, do you turn to the word of God to regain your confidence?

Do you realize that we have a high priest that is able to sympathize with our weakness?

> **Prayer:** Lord, thank You for being a God that can comfort and sympathize with our weakness and who can instruct us in the way we should go. A God that loves us no matter what is going on in our lives.

CHAPTER 42

THE WORD CHANGES EVERYTHING

MY GIFTS HAVE POWER

THE WORD CHANGES EVERYTHING

Your Gifts will make room for you and put you before great people!
Proverbs 18:16

It is important to recognize that every person has unique talents and abilities, which are often referred to as "gifts." These gifts can range from artistic talents to athletic abilities to exceptional problem-solving skills. Regardless of what they are, our gifts are powerful tools that we can use to make a positive impact on the world around us.

Embrace your strengths: Take the time to reflect on your gifts and acknowledge the strengths That God has blessed you with. Recognize the unique abilities that set you apart and make you special. Embrace them, and don't be afraid to showcase them. Our gifts allow us to shine and give God the glory for the magnificent gifts He has given us.

Use your gifts to make a difference: Identify how your gifts can be used to make a positive impact in your community or in the world. Whether it's volunteering your time, using your creativity to inspire others, or mentoring someone who can benefit from your expertise, your gifts have the power to create change.

Believe in yourself: Trust in your abilities and the power of your gifts given to you by God. Don't be afraid to take risks or step outside of your comfort zone. Choose to talk and walk by faith. Believe that you have what it takes to succeed and use your gifts to bring life to your dreams.

Share your gifts with others: Don't keep your gifts to yourself. Share them with others and inspire them to embrace their own gifts. You never know how your gifts can positively impact someone else's life.

THE WORD CHANGES EVERYTHING

In conclusion, remember that your gifts have power, and with that power comes great responsibility. Use your gifts wisely and always strive to make a positive impact on the world around you.

Are you willing to share your Gifts with others?

Do you feel like you embrace your gifts?

Do you believe in yourself, and the power God has given you?

Are you using your gifts to make a difference in the world?

> **Prayer:** Lord, thank You for showing me that my gifts have the power to change my life. Thank You for the guidance that You give me each and every day. Thank You for teaching me how to trust the process that You are taking me through each and every day.

CHAPTER 43

THE WORD CHANGES EVERYTHING

MY GOD DOES NOT CHANGE

THE WORD CHANGES EVERYTHING

> "I The Lord do not change. So, you O' descendants of Jacob are not destroyed. Malachi 3:6

According to Christian belief, God is immutable, which means that He does not change. This belief is based on several passages in the Bible that suggest that God is unchanging and consistent in His nature.

One such passage is found in the book of Malachi 3:6, where God says, "For I the Lord do not change; therefore you, O children of Jacob, are not consumed."

This passage emphasizes that God's nature is unchanging, and this is why His people are not destroyed despite their sins and shortcomings.

Another passage that emphasizes God's unchanging nature is found in the New Testament in the book of James 1:17, which says, "Every good gift and every perfect gift is from above, coming down from the Father of lights, with whom there is no variation or shadow due to change." This passage highlights that God's goodness and generosity are consistent and unchanging.

The idea of God's immutability also has theological implications for Christian belief. For example, it is believed that God's unchanging nature guarantees the reliability of His promises and the truthfulness of His word. If God were subject to change, then His promises and word could not be trusted.

Furthermore, God's immutability provides a source of comfort and stability for Christians. In a world that is constantly changing, Christians believe that they can depend on God's unchanging nature and character.

THE WORD CHANGES EVERYTHING

This belief provides a sense of security and peace, knowing that they can trust in God's steadfast love and faithfulness, even in the midst of difficult circumstances.

In conclusion, Christians believe that God does not change, and that this belief is supported by various passages in the Bible. God's unchanging nature is seen as a source of stability, reliability, and comfort for believers, and it has important theological implications for Christian doctrine.

THE WORD CHANGES EVERYTHING

Do you trust the fact that God does not change?

How confident do you feel about God's unchanging Hand?

How confident are you in the power of God?

What is your understanding of Malachi 3:6?

Prayer: Lord, thank You for helping me to understand the importance of Your unchanging love towards me. Thank You for showing me that I can trust You for all eternity.

CHAPTER 44

THE WORD CHANGES EVERYTHING

MY GOD IS WORKING ALL THINGS OUT FOR ME

THE WORD CHANGES EVERYTHING

> And we know that all things work together for those who love the Lord and are called according to His purpose. Romans 8:28

The belief that God works all things together for our good is rooted in the Christian faith and is based on the teachings of the Bible. This concept can be found in the book of Romans, chapter 8, verse 28, which says, "And we know that all things work together for good to them that love God, to them who are the called according to his purpose."

This verse suggests that everything that happens in our lives, both good and bad, can ultimately lead to our benefit if we love God and follow his plan for our lives. It does not mean that everything that happens to us is good, nor does it mean that we will always understand or see the good in every situation. However, it encourages us to have faith in God's wisdom and sovereignty, knowing that he can use even the difficult and painful experiences we face to shape us into the people He wants us to be.

One of the key aspects of this concept is the importance of trusting God, even when things don't seem to make sense or when we don't understand why something is happening. When we trust in God, we can have peace and confidence, knowing that He is in control and has our best interests at heart. This can help us to face challenges and difficulties with greater resilience and faith, knowing that God is working on our behalf.

It's important to note that this concept doesn't mean that we should passively accept every negative circumstance in our lives without taking action to improve our situation or help others. Instead, it encourages us to approach every situation with a positive attitude, seeking to find the good in every circumstance and looking for ways to use our experiences to grow, learn, and help others.

THE WORD CHANGES EVERYTHING

In summary, the belief that God works all things together for our good is a powerful and comforting idea that can help us to face the ups and downs of life with faith, hope, and resilience. By trusting in God's wisdom and sovereignty, we can find meaning and purpose in every situation and use our experiences to grow closer to Him and make a positive impact on the world around us.

THE WORD CHANGES EVERYTHING

One of the key aspects of this concept is the importance of trusting God, even when things don't seem to make sense or when we don't understand why something is happening. What are your thoughts?

God encourages us to have faith in His wisdom and sovereignty, knowing that He can use even the difficult situations and experiences we face to shape us into the people He wants us to be. What are your thoughts?

We should not passively accept every negative circumstance in our lives without taking action to improve our situation. We should seek the guidance of God to see us through. What are your thoughts?

Do you see God working all things together in your life or your situation?

> **Prayer:** Lord, thank You for working all things out for me even when I can't see the direction You are taking me. Thank You for showing me the importance of keeping my eyes on You at all times and not my circumstances.

CHAPTER 45

THE WORD CHANGES EVERYTHING

MY HELP COMES FROM THE LORD

THE WORD CHANGES EVERYTHING

> I will lift up mine eyes unto the hills from where cometh my help. My help cometh from the Lord, which made heaven and earth.
> Psalms 121:1

"My help comes from the Lord" is a powerful statement of faith and trust in God's provision and protection. Here are some key points we can learn from this statement:

Trust in God's Sovereignty: When we say, "My help comes from the Lord," we acknowledge that God is in control and has the power to help us. We trust in his sovereignty over our lives and situations.

Seek God's Help First: The phrase "My help comes from the Lord" suggests that we should seek God's help first before seeking help from other sources. This means turning to prayer, seeking guidance from the Bible, and seeking counsel from wise and godly people.

God is Our Source of Strength: When we say, "My help comes from the Lord," we recognize that God is our ultimate source of strength. We can't do everything on our own, and we need His strength to help us through difficult times.

We Can Depend on God's Faithfulness: The phrase "My help comes from the Lord" also reminds us that God is faithful and will always be there for us. We can depend on him to provide for our needs and protect us from harm.

Let Go of Fear and Anxiety: When we trust in God and say, "My help comes from the Lord," we can let go of fear and anxiety. We know that God is with us and will help us through whatever challenges we may face.

THE WORD CHANGES EVERYTHING

In summary, the phrase "My help comes from the Lord" is a powerful statement of faith and trust in God's provision and protection. It reminds us to trust in God's sovereignty, seek His help first, depend on his strength, trust in His faithfulness, trust in His understanding. and let go of fear and anxiety.

How open are you to trusting in the sovereignty of the Lord?

Do you seek God first before making any major decisions?

How is depending on God's strength been a help to you in times of difficulty?

What is the importance of releasing all fear and anxiety to the Lord?

> **Prayer:** Lord, thank You for helping me to release all my fear and anxieties into Your hands where I can be reassured that You will be faithful to take care of them.

CHAPTER 46
THE WORD CHANGES EVERYTHING

MY LIGHT IS SHINING BRIGHTLY

THE WORD CHANGES EVERYTHING

> Let your light so shine before men that they may see your moral excellence and your praiseworthy, noble, and good deeds and recognize and honor and praise and glorify your Father Who is Heaven.
> Matthew 5:16

Letting your light shine brightly before the Lord is an important lesson that teaches us to live a life that honors God and reflects His glory. This lesson is based on the words of Jesus in Matthew 5:16, where He says, "Let your light shine before others, so that they may see your good works and give glory to your Father in heaven."

The "light" that Jesus is referring to here is the good works that we do as followers of Christ. These good works can include things like showing kindness and compassion to others, sharing the Gospel, serving those in need, and living a life that is pleasing to God.

When we let our light shine brightly before the Lord, we are not seeking to draw attention to ourselves or to receive praise from others. Instead, we are seeking to glorify God and to point others to Him. We are acknowledging that everything good that we do comes from Him and that we want to use our lives to bring Him honor and praise.

Letting our light shine brightly also means that we are not afraid to stand up for what is right and to speak out against injustice and evil. We are willing to be a witness for Christ in a world that desperately needs to hear His message of hope and salvation.

In summary, letting our light shine brightly before the Lord means living a life that reflects His love, grace, and truth. It means using our gifts and talents to serve others and to bring glory to God. And it means being a

THE WORD CHANGES EVERYTHING

witness for Christ in everything that we do so that others may come to know Him and give Him the praise and honor that He deserves.

Are you allowing the light of Jesus Christ to shine brightly within you?

What do you think God meant in Matthew 5:16?

Are you confident in sharing the Gospel?

Do you study the Bible? If not, why?

> **Prayer:** Lord, help me to understand Your word. Give me an understanding of it so that I may share it with others. Help me to listen and pay attention to Your voice. Lord, give me the confidence to share with others what You have done for me.

CHAPTER 47

THE WORD CHANGES EVERYTHING

MY LORD IS STRONG AND MIGHTY

THE WORD CHANGES EVERYTHING

Lift up your heads, O ye gates; and be lifted up, you age-abiding doors, that the King of glory may come in. Who is the King of glory? The Lord strong and mighty, the Lord mighty in battle. Psalm 24:7-8

The Lord is indeed strong and mighty, and there are countless examples throughout history and in the Bible that demonstrate His power and might.

God is the Creator: One of the clearest examples of God's strength and might is found in the story of creation in the book of Genesis. By His very words, God brought the universe and all life into existence. His power is beyond measure, and nothing is impossible for Him.

God parted the Red Sea: In the book of Exodus, we read how God parted the Red Sea so that the Israelites could escape from Pharaoh's army. This was a miraculous event that demonstrated God's power over nature and His ability to protect His people.

God defeated Goliath: In the story of David and Goliath, we see how God empowered a young shepherd boy to defeat a giant warrior. David's victory was not because of his own strength or skill but because of God's power and might.

Jesus' Resurrection: The ultimate display of God's strength and might is seen in the resurrection of Jesus Christ. Death could not hold Him down, and He rose from the grave, conquering sin and death. This event demonstrates God's power over the greatest enemy of all.

Our daily lives: Even in our daily lives, we can see God's strength and might at work. He sustains us, protects us, and provides for us. We can rely on His power to guide us through difficult times and to give us hope for the future.

In conclusion, the Lord is indeed strong and mighty, and His power is evident in all aspects of life. We can trust in His strength and rely on His might to guide us through life's challenges and to give us hope for the future.

THE WORD CHANGES EVERYTHING

How do you see God's strength and power moving in your own life?

What does the resurrection of Christ's death mean to you?

How do you see the strength and mighty power of God in the story of David and Goliath?

What are some of the Goliaths in your life? How did you slay them?

Prayer: Lord, thank You for taking down the Goliaths in my life. Thank You for making the ultimate sacrifice for me on Calvary. Thank You for showing up strong and mighty in my life.

CHAPTER 48

THE WORD CHANGES EVERYTHING

MY LORD'S MERCY ENDURES FOREVER

> O give thank to the Lord, for He is good; for His mercy and loving-kindness endure forever. O give thanks to the God of gods for His mercy and loving-kindness endure forever. And rescued us from our enemies, for His and loving-kindness endure forever; Psalms 136:1, 2, 24

The Lord's mercy enduring forever is a concept that is found throughout the Bible. It is a testament to God's unfailing love and grace towards humanity. Here are some key points that can help understand this concept better:

God's mercy is infinite: The Bible states that God's mercy is eternal, and it endures forever. This means that no matter what we do or how far we may have strayed from Him, God's love and grace are always available to us.

It is not dependent on our works: God's mercy is not something we can earn through our good deeds or righteous acts. It is a free gift that is offered to all who seek it.

It is available to all: God's mercy is not limited to a particular group of people. It is available to everyone, regardless of race, gender, or social status.

It is demonstrated in the life, death, and resurrection of Jesus Christ: The ultimate demonstration of God's mercy is found in the life, death, and resurrection of Jesus Christ. Through his sacrifice, we are offered forgiveness and redemption, and we can be reconciled to God.
We are called to extend mercy to others: As recipients of God's mercy, we are called to extend mercy to others. This means showing kindness, compassion, and forgiveness, even to those who may not deserve it.

THE WORD CHANGES EVERYTHING

In summary, the Lord's mercy endures forever and is a reminder of God's unending love and grace toward humanity. It is a call to us to seek His mercy and extend it to others. For God loves the sinner He just doesn't love the sin.

Did you know that God's mercy is not based on your good deeds?

Did you know that God's mercy is available to all of us?

Do you see the importance of offering mercy to others?

Did you realize that God loves us as sinners but not our sins?

> **Prayer:** Lord, thank You for Your love and Your mercy. Thank You for caring for me and wanting me to be all that You have called me to be. Thank You for showing me that all things are possible through Your loving kindness.

CHAPTER 49

THE WORD CHANGES EVERYTHING

MY LORD WILL ALWAYS BE WITH ME

THE WORD CHANGES EVERYTHING

No man shall be able to stand before you all the days of your life. As I was with Moses, so I will be with you; I will not fail you or forsake you.
Joshua 1:5

God is omnipresent: One of the most important teachings as Christians is that God is omnipresent, meaning that He is present everywhere at all times. This means that no matter where you go or what you do, God is always with you.

God is faithful: Another key teaching is that God is faithful and will always keep His promises. This means that if you trust in God and seek His guidance, He will be with you and guide you through life's challenges.

Prayer and meditation can help you feel God's presence: Prayer and meditation are powerful tools that can help you connect with God and feel His presence. By taking time to reflect on your relationship with God and express your thoughts and feelings, you can strengthen your faith and sense of connection with this mighty and powerful God.

Trust in God's plan: Finally, it's important to remember that God has a plan for your life and is always working for your good, even if you can't see it at the moment. By trusting in God's plan and surrendering your will to His, you can find peace and comfort in the knowledge that He is always with you.

Overall, the lesson is that if you have faith in God and seek His guidance through prayer and meditation, you can be assured that He will always be with you, guiding you through life's challenges and helping you to fulfill the purpose that He has for you.

THE WORD CHANGES EVERYTHING

How do you think you could learn to trust God more?

Do you feel you could spend more time meditating on God's word and spending more time with Him in prayer?

How faithfully do you seek God?

What does God's omnipresence mean in your life?

> **Prayer:** Lord, thank You for being ever present in my life. Thank You for always showing up in my life. Thank You for showing me how much I can trust in You to always be there for me.

CHAPTER 50

THE WORD CHANGES EVERYTHING

MY MIND IS RENEWED

THE WORD CHANGES EVERYTHING

Do not be conformed to the patterns this world, but be transformed by the renewing of your mind Romans 12:2

According to the Bible, the mind is a powerful part of our being that plays a crucial role in our spiritual growth and transformation. In Romans 12:2, the apostle Paul writes, "Do not be conformed to this world, but be transformed by the renewing of your mind, that you may prove what is that good and acceptable and perfect will of God."

Renewing the mind involves a process of transformation from the inside out, where our thoughts and beliefs are changed by the power of God. This process is not automatic, but it requires intentional effort on our part to align our thoughts with God's truth and to resist the lies and distractions of the world.

Here are some key lessons on how to renew the mind from a biblical point of view.

Recognize the need for renewal: We all have thoughts and beliefs that are shaped by our upbringing, culture, and personal experiences. Some of these thoughts may not be aligned with God's truth, and we need to be aware of them to begin the process of transformation.

Immerse yourself in God's Word: The Bible is the ultimate source of truth that reveals God's character, will, and promises. Reading, studying, and meditating on the Scriptures can help us renew our minds and align our thoughts with God's truth.

Pray for wisdom and guidance: The Holy Spirit is our helper and guide who can give us understanding and discernment to recognize the lies of the enemy and to embrace God's truth.

Surround yourself with Godly influences: Our thoughts and beliefs can be influenced by the people we spend time with. Surrounding ourselves with people who are committed to following God and His truth can help us renew our minds and stay focused on Him.

Practice self-control: Renewing the mind involves replacing old thought patterns and behaviors with new ones that reflect God's truth. This requires self-discipline and the willingness to let go of things that are not beneficial for our spiritual growth.

In summary, renewing the mind is a crucial part of our spiritual growth as believers. By immersing ourselves in God's Word, praying for wisdom and guidance, surrounding ourselves with godly influences, and practicing self-control, we can experience transformation and live a life that reflects God's truth and glory.

THE WORD CHANGES EVERYTHING

What do you do to renew your mind daily?

Do you realize that renewing your mind is a crucial part of your spiritual growth?

How do to practice self-control?

Do you have Godly influences around you?

> **Prayer:** Lord, thank You for helping me see the importance of renewing my mind. Thank You for helping me see that immersing myself in your word will help me to renew my mind. Thank you for showing me the importance of having a Godly influence in my life.

WORDS TO ENCOURAGE YOU ON YOUR JOURNEY. REPEAT THEM EVERY MORNING!

Philippians 4:6-7
I will not be anxious about anything; instead in everything through prayer and petition with thanksgiving, I will tell my request to God.
In the name and through the power of Jesus Christ!

John 16:23-24
My Father will give me whatever I ask in His name. I will ask and I will receive, and my joy will be completed.
In the name and through the power of Jesus Christ!

Proverbs 10:22
The blessings of the Lord make me rich, and He adds no sorrow with it.
In the name and through the power of Jesus Christ!

THE WORD CHANGES EVERYTHING

Psalm 32:8
The Lord will instruct me and teach me in the way I should go. He will council and watch over me. He will guide me with His eyes.
In the name and through the power of Jesus Christ!

Jeremiah 31:3
In a far off land the Lord will manifest Himself to me. He will say to me (put your name here), I have loved you with everlasting love. That is why I continue to be faithful to you.
In the name and through the power of Jesus Christ!

Ephesians 6:16
I will take up the shield of faith with which I can extinguish all the flaming arrows of the enemy!
In the name and through the power of Jesus Christ!

Matthew 6:33
I will seek first the kingdom of God and His righteousness. When I do that, all things shall be added to me.
In the name and through the power of Jesus Christ!

Proverbs 3:5-6
I will trust in the Lord with all my heart and lean not on my own understanding; I will acknowledge you in all your ways, for it is You that will make my paths straight.
In the name and through the power of Jesus Christ!

Psalm 139:14
I praise You because I am fearfully and wonderfully made; by you, your works are wonderful, and I know them full well.
In the name and through the power of Jesus Christ!

THE WORD CHANGES EVERYTHING

Romans 12:2
I will not be conformed to the patterns of this world, but I will be transformed by the renewal of my mind. Then I will know God's good and pleasing and perfect will for my life.
In the name and through the power of Jesus Christ!

Psalm 37:7
I wait patiently on the Lord. I wait confidently for Him.
In the name and through the power of Jesus Christ!

Psalm 21:6
For You grant me lasting blessings. You gave me great joy by allowing me into your presence!
In the name and through the power of Jesus Christ!

Hebrews 4:16
Therefore, I will confidently approach the throne of favor, to receive mercy and favor whenever I need help.
In the name and through the power of Jesus Christ!

QUOTES TO INSPIRE YOU

"Think like a queen. A queen is not afraid to fail. Failure is another stepping stone to greatness." Oprah Winfrey

"You were designed for accomplishment, engineered for success, and endowed with the seeds of greatness." Zig Ziglar

"Never underestimate the power of dreams and the influence of the human spirit. We are all the same in this notion: the potential for greatness lives within each of us." Wilma Rudolph

"Greatness is not measured by what a woman accomplishes, but by the opposition she has overcome to reach her goal." Dorothy Height

"You are destined for greatness. Believe in yourself and go for it. Greatness comes by surrounding yourself with great people."
Alahdal A. Hussein

"Be not afraid of greatness. Some are born great, some achieve greatness, and others have greatness thrust upon them." William Shakespeare

THE WORD CHANGES EVERYTHING

"Great things in business are never done by one person. They're done by a team of people." Steve Jobs

"Greatness is inside all of us, but first we must choose to be great." Nora Shariff Borden

"Greatness comes from the desire to do extraordinary things." Nora Shariff Borden

"Don't limit yourself. Many people limit themselves to what they think they can do. You can go as far your mind lets you. What you believe, remember you can achieve." Mary Kay Ash

"Great thoughts speak only to the thoughtful mind, but great actions speak to all mankind." Theodore Roosevelt

"If we cannot see the possibility of greatness, how can we dream it?" Lee Strasberg

"Keep away from people who try to belittle your ambitions. Small people always do that, but the really great make you feel that you, too, can become great." Mark Twain

"A woman's greatness is all she needs to hold on to when opposition shows up." Nora Shariff Borden

'When you speak greatness into the lives of others, greatness will come back to you." Nora Shariff Borden.

"Great things happen when people have Great expectations." Nora Shariff Borden

THE WORD CHANGES EVERYTHING

"Great things happen when you believe they can." Nora Shariff Borden
"No matter who you are, greatness awaits you. All you have do is believe and walk in it." Nora Shariff Borden

"If you're walking down the right path and you're willing to keep walking, eventually you'll make progress." President Barack Obama

"Whatever is bringing you down, get rid of it. Because you'll find that when you're free, your true self comes out." Tina Turner

"Every great dream begins with a dreamer. Always remember: you have within you the strength, the patience, and the passion to reach for the stars to change the world." Harriet Tubman

"Greatness occurs when your children love you, when your critics respect you, and when you have peace of mind." Quincy Jones

"A made up mind can do anything. All you have to do is decide what you want." Nora Shariff Borden

"Always stay true to yourself and never let what somebody else says distract you from your goals." Michelle Obama

"Always be careful of your circle of influence. The right circle can lift you up, and the wrong circle can weigh you down!" Nora Shariff Borden

"If you don't like something, change it. If you can't change it, change your attitude." Maya Angelou

THE WORD CHANGES EVERYTHING

"I have come to believe over and over again that what is most important to me must be spoken, made verbal and shared, even at the risk of having it bruised or misunderstood." Audre Lorde

"No one should negotiate their dreams. Dreams must be free to flee and fly high. You should never surrender your dreams." Jesse Jackson

"Just don't give up what you're trying to do. Where there is love and inspiration, I don't think you can go wrong." Ella Fitzgerald

"It's not the load that breaks you down. It's the way you carry it." Lena Horne

"Have a Vision. Be demanding." Colin Powell

"You're obligated to win. You're obligated to keep trying to do the best you can every day." Marian Wright Edelman

"I have learned over the years that when one's mind is made up, this diminishes fear; knowing what must be done does away with fear." Rosa Parks

"Sometimes, what you're looking for is already there." Aretha Franklin

"When you are seeking to bring big plans to fruition, it is important with whom you regularly associate." Mark Twain

www.ingramcontent.com/pod-product-compliance
Lightning Source LLC
Chambersburg PA
CBHW051545010526
44118CB00022B/2582